the **NO-NONSENSE** guide to

GLOBAL MEDIA

Peter Steven

D0424569

'Publishers have created lists of short books
that discuss the questions that your average
[electoral] candidate will only ever touch if
armed with a slogan and a soundbite. Together
[such books] hint at a resurgence of the grand
educational tradition... Closest to the hot
headline issues are *The No-Nonsense Guides*.
These target those topics that a large army of
voters care about, but that politicos evade.
Arguments, figures and documents combine to
prove that good journalism is far too important
to be left to (most) journalists.'

Boyd Tonkin,
The Independent,
London

The No-Nonsense Guide to Global Media
First published in the UK by
New Internationalist™ Publications Ltd
55 Rectory Road
Oxford OX4 1BW, UK
www.newint.org
New Internationalist is a registered trade mark.

In association with
Verso
6 Meard Street,
London
W1F 0EG
www.versobooks.com

Cover image: Larry Williams / Corbis

Design by Ian Nixon / New Internationalist Publications Ltd.

Printed by TJ International Ltd, Padstow, Cornwall, UK.

British Library Cataloguing-in-Publication Data.
A catalogue record for this book is available from the British Library.

Library of Congress Cataloguing-in-Publication Data.
A catalogue for this book is available from the Library of Congress.

ISBN 1-85984-581-9

the NO-NONSENSE guide to

GLOBAL MEDIA

Peter Steven

Acknowledgements

Thank you to all the people in Chapter One who shared their thoughts about living with the media. Special thanks to Blaine Allan, Matt Adams, Jonathan Barker, Wayne Ellwood, Harry Glasbeek, Steve Izma, Chuck Kleinhans, Marilyn Legge, Sally Miller, Christine Morris, Geraldine Sadoway and Richard Swift for their indispensable comments and support. The book and the arguments within were greatly improved through the skilled and sensitive editing and guidance of Katharine Ainger and Troth Wells at the *New Internationalist*.

Dedication

To Geri, for her ongoing support, and to Charlie and Sam, already living with the media and struggling to separate the wheat from the chaff.

About the author

Peter Steven has written on many aspects of cinema, history and social change. He is the author of *Brink of Reality: New Canadian Documentary Film and Video* and *Jump Cut: Hollywood, Politics and Counter-Cinema,* a regular contributor to the *New Internationalist*, and an associate editor of *Jump Cut magazine. He lives in Toronto.*

Other titles in the series

The No-Nonsense Guide to Globalization
The No-Nonsense Guide to Fair Trade
The No-Nonsense Guide to Climate Change
The No-Nonsense Guide to International Migration
The No-Nonsense Guide to Sexual Diversity
The No-Nonsense Guide to World History
The No-Nonsense Guide to Democracy
The No-Nonsense Guide to Class, Caste and Hierarchies
The No-Nonsense Guide to the Arms Trade
The No-Nonsense Guide to International Development
The No-Nonsense Guide to Indigenous Peoples
The No-Nonsense Guide to Terrorism
The No-Nonsense Guide to HIV/AIDS
The No-Nonsense Guide to World Poverty
The No-Nonsense Guide to Islam

Foreword

PETER STEVEN IS a surprisingly enlightened Western media academic. In contrast to many others in the domain, he is remarkably aware that the Western males' reflection takes up most of the mirror-space of what media studies deems noteworthy. On the whole, media theory places anything identified as *other* as an appendage or incorporates it into the dominant view of reality, and of how the world should be. Feminist theory has contributed significantly to reshaping that closeted view. However, it is still a view that stems from a tradition of rationalism and crusader values, that at best aims to 'save' the downtrodden, rather than ratifying the perfectly valid reality and value system of the *other*.

Undertaking the enormous task of intellectually compressing the subject of global media into this short *No-Nonsense Guide* is as amazing a feat as that of digital technology itself. However, such compression could lead the writer to believe they are enabling the masses to reflect on how they are controlled by political totalitarianism through the dominant media. But Steven questions this task and from his subtle analyses one can comprehend the ways in which we can be imprisoned. Our imprisonment is made up of the illusion of freedom of speech constructed and maintained by digital walls consisting of data, images, sounds, intellectual junk mail and most importantly the proliferation of the English language.

But as we move through Steven's compelling book, he shows us alternative ways of viewing media by focusing not solely on the technology itself but on its development. As he reveals, economic globalization does not automatically mean a globalization of cultures. Does mass media forge diversity or 'homogenization'; or is it the perpetuation of class disguised as the search for happiness? Steven prompts us to question our roles not only as audience but also artists. He raises, and encourages us to do likewise, the question of how the media reflects society: are we passive recipients, or do we have a part in constructing the world? Is the media just a reflection of what amounts to low-grade programming and superficial relationships between people existing in an imposed world? Are we just subjects primed to accept all the new objects devised by technological wizardry? In his final chapter he provides some sound ideas and actions for change as well as hope.

The media, as Steven demonstrates, is an advocate to be befriended as it can empower us to reveal the hidden parts of the nature of the universe, rather than an instrument to control or be controlled by. Non-Western countries are trying to demonstrate through their cultural interpretation and use of the media that it is merely another technique of communication and not the bearer of freedom of speech or the truth or liberty, as the West believes.

Steven's range of wonderful stories makes a significant contribution, by enlightening readers about the many and varying ways in which the media is, and can be, used to satisfy our needs. These needs ultimately can either imprison us in a commodified matrix of a reality that only benefits the few, or assist us to bring to the fore the hidden wonders of the globe for the enjoyment of all. Perhaps the media can be considered a Pandora's Box full of wonders and challenges, and it behoves everyone to respond both creatively and responsibly for the benefit of all.

Christine Morris

Christine Morris is a traditional custodian of Aboriginal Law from the Kombumerri/Mununjahlai clans and a research fellow at Griffith University, Brisbane, Australia.

the **NO-NONSENSE** guide to

GLOBAL MEDIA
Peter Steven

CONTENTS

the NO-NONSENSE guide to

GLOBAL MEDIA

A FEW MONTHS back I sent out a small question-naire to several people around the world. The diverse voices in Chapter One belong to those who were kind enough to write back. In my questions I had asked if they would speak in concrete terms about their engagement with various forms of media.

Each person who replied hit me with little surpris-es, like Christine Morris's reference to the 'dolly-pink dollar' of young Australian girls' spending power, the fact that Professor Manjunath Pendakur's college newspaper is called the Daily Egyptian, or that 'Dogtown Saloon' is a bluegrass radio program on the internet. The comments also provide many tantalizing leads to follow, such as Celina Del Felice's reference to La Red Joven in Argentina, or Olivia Ward's recom-mendation of The Johnson List for stories on Russia.

What emerges in these voices from around the world sets the stage for the main theme of the book. I wanted to show the incredible power and reach of the dominant media – the homogenized, commercial, mono-media that most of us share. Yet at the same time I hoped to call up the diverse, alternative, sometimes local, sometimes international forms of media in oppo-sition struggling for space. As a student of international media I am not prepared to give up on either the dom-inant or the alternative sides of the media equation. It is politically dangerous and elitist to write off all forms of dominant media and their audiences as hopelessly retrograde. At the same time we must offer all the sup-port and encouragement possible to those producers and audiences pushing to create other forms.

The book starts out with the big, ominous forces of global media now facing us. We can not underestimate the power and brute force behind the barons of global media, the Rupert Murdochs and Silvio Berlusconis of the world who wield political and economic power as well as the ability to shape dreams through our entertainment. An understanding of this media power in both the news and entertainment sectors is vital both politically and culturally if we hope to achieve democratic change.

At the same time the wide range of specific media forms are not simple types of communication or propaganda. They are symbolic representations of people, ideas and realities, with multiple meanings. And these meanings take final shape only through contact with specific audiences. They become meanings that can't be totally controlled. The media may be cultural industries but they also operate in the realm of media art.

The book ends with a chapter of ideas for moving forward. Above all I hope that readers will agree that although the media may be dominant they are not omnipotent. In the words of the social activist and teacher Ben Carniol, 'Don't accept the TINA situation that we're always fed; you know, TINA, There Is No Alternative.' Think forward to a better media world.

Peter Steven
Toronto

1 Living with the media – voices across the world

People from around the world describe their personal experiences of diverse media, both local and global.

WHEN I STARTED writing this book I knew it would be important to discover what people in different parts of the world were watching, hearing and reading. Some of that media is homogenized by the dominant monoculture, some locally produced and incredibly diverse.

Manjunath Prendakur, Carbondale, USA / Karnataka, India

My first encounter with the movies was at a 'touring talkies' in a small village in Karnataka when I was eight years old. In the 1950s I saw many films in the tent theatre – a swashbuckler film, *Neela Malai Thirudan* (Tamil); a folktale, *Malleeswari* (Telugu); a social commentary, *Kanyadana* (Kannada); a mythological film, *Bhakta Prahallada* (Kannada); and an historical film, *Jhansi Ki Rani* (Hindi).

I listen to Indian film and classical music on the radio and I hear jazz and alternative music on a student-operated station called WIDB in Carbondale. I get Indian films from netflix.com.

I subscribe to *The Daily Egyptian,* our student produced paper; online I read *The Hindu, Indian Express* and *Filmfare.* The coverage of the war on Iraq is a cause for concern among a lot of people.

Christine Morris, Brisbane, Australia

I like to read *The Koori Mail,* the only indigenous paper with an indigenous editor. The format is different as it prides itself more on the images than the text. Indigenous people want to see images of their own people.

We are fortunate to have a variety of independent film theatres. This has allowed for more films by indigenous directors such as *One Night the Moon,* by Rachel Perkins and *Atanarjuat: the Fast Runner,* by Zach Kunuk.

For my family and the general population, the dolly-pink dollar relating to female youth is well represented – no surprise considering females of the dominant cultures are the most researched group in Australia.

Urvashi Butalia, New Delhi, India
Should films be financed by crooks? That is the biggest controversy here. Film stars are often threatened by the underworld. Recently, one woman spoke out and the papers were full of her courage.

For the very young children it's cartoons and *The National Geographic* when there are animal programs. The young women watch Indian films and *Friends* on TV. But they are very choosy and look for their favorite actors. In the first week of August we watched the local serials, *Kasauti, Sanjeevani,* a medical serial and the news.

There is a huge public debate in the women's movement about censorship and the expression of women's sexuality on television. We particularly talk about how gender is reflected in our programmes. I am part of a monitoring group which gives constant feedback to media people.

Valerie Wint, Toronto, Canada / Kingston, Jamaica
When I left Jamaica in 1985, we had only two FM radio stations and one TV station, only on air from four pm to midnight. Now, my mother pulls in BBC, CNN and CITY TV from Toronto, and the local newscasts plus African and other regional sources.

Everyone has a cell phone, even the little guy selling coconuts on the beach.

Kole Shettima, Lagos, Nigeria / Washington, DC, USA
In Nigeria right now there is debate that some of the music in Hausa home videos is heavily influenced by Indian culture. The Government banned Femi Kuti's show on TV because it is 'promoting nudity'.

I watch TV news: the BBC, CNN, and the Nigerian Television Authority

Olivia Ward, Canada/England/Russia
I have recently read *The Life of My Choosing*, by Wilfred Thesiger, *The Fall of the House of Saud*, by Said Aburish and *Alice in Exile* by Piers Paul Read.

The book-publishing mergers are a problem and getting more so. Also the swallowing of independent bookstores by chains which in Canada has reduced the number of unusual books considerably. One of my favorite places is the Toronto Women's Bookstore.

Many of my friends and colleagues are in the media and I always scan their work – Suzy Goldenberg at *The Guardian*, Annie Garrels at National Public Radio, Robert Fisk at *The Independent*. I subscribe to several online services such as *Truthout*, *The Johnson List* (for Russian stories), *The Institute for War and Peace Reporting* (for the Balkans and Mideast).

Sally Miller, Toronto, Canada
I use Google News, and then connect to articles from hundreds of different papers through that. I also check on environmental news at sites like 'PlanetArk' and 'Greenpeace'.

Although the internet still represents to some extent the free access and global communications that everyone is so excited about, increasingly it certainly inflicts more fees and more irritating advertising on the viewer.

I listen to CBC's 'Sound Advice', and on internet radio: 'Dogtown Saloon', WUMB, and 'Killer Rabbit' for bluegrass, roots and folk music.

Celina Del Felice, Rosario, Argentina

Right now I'm listening to Argentine folk music – Chacarera, Peteco, Carabajal and Pedro Guerra.

We are very proud of our local and national film production. After the devaluation of our currency in 2002 many filmmakers are coming to Buenos Aires to shoot because of the quality of the technicians, good locations, and so forth.

I subscribe to *La Capital*, Rosario, *Clarin*, Buenos Aires, *El Pais*, Spain. And also the online news service, *La Red Joven*.

2 Global media

The world's media flow increases at an ever-faster rate, surrounding our lives with images, sounds, data and noise. But some have more media than others, and all of us interpret it differently based on our own experience. Economic globalization is causing the consolidation of the world's giant media companies, but the globalization of culture does not follow automatically.

MATT GRIPPED THE phone and paced the floor of his modest, slightly tattered office. After ten calls and a dozen emails he had finally hit on a sure-fire method to make contact and deliver his request. Michael Moore would finally be reached.

Moore, the left-wing gadfly and author of *Stupid White Men*, had been on the road for weeks and was hard to pin down. The book had soared to the top of the US best-seller lists – college and town-hall audiences were clamoring to hear his analysis and see his trademark political standup routine. Even the talk shows, Oprah, Barbara Walters, Connie Chung and *Seattle This Morning*, were calling. In Britain, *Stupid White Men* had sold out of its first print run before the book was even released.

Moore had written a brilliant exercise in what Hollywood might dub 'High Concept', something so clear and simple that it captures attention and imaginations immediately. Though some critics found the analysis a little thin and slipshod, its exposé of corporate greed, government sleaze and shrinking democracy in the US had struck a deep chord among huge numbers of book buyers, many new to a left critique of US society. But the surge to number one had almost died in infancy. Moore had sold his book to HarperCollins, one of the largest and most powerful publishers in the world, owned by the right-wing crusader and billionaire

Rupert Murdoch. Murdoch was not averse to meddling if his interests were affected. Five years earlier he had quashed a publishing deal between HarperCollins and Chris Patten, the former Governor of Hong Kong, for a book critical of mainland China. The timing was bad. Murdoch was working in a new partnership with the Chinese Government to extend the reach of his Star TV satellite empire and Patten's book would surely cause trouble.

In a similar fashion, Moore's book almost died when HarperCollins tried to shelve it after September 11. But with the help of many sympathetic librarians, Moore – true to his pugnacious style and genius for publicity – had managed to expose the political bias of the publisher. They were embarrassed enough to relent and had to settle for reaping the subsequent, huge profits.

That's the kind of creative politics that Matt loved. A popular, hard-hitting book written by a colorful, outspoken activist. Matt got off the phone and explained the situation to our small group in Toronto. Moore was about to speak that night at Cornell University in Ithaca, New York. Matt's friend Joe was on the organizing committee and had agreed to speak with Moore on our behalf. Would Moore accept our invitation to speak in Toronto as part of our LeftWords book festival? Could he talk the corporate types at HarperCollins' Toronto office into letting us serve as hosts rather than handing the event to the mainstream organization they had set up? Surely as a grassroots activist Moore would hear our pitch and see the political appeal, we thought. The next day Joe reported in. Moore had inspired another sellout crowd. According to Joe, he had listened carefully to our invitation and taken our package of background materials.

Three weeks later it was all over. Michael Moore had come to Toronto and gone, ripping through a brilliant performance and providing a much needed radical critique that probably inspired many to get involved.

But Matt had heard no more – the marketing department at HarperCollins had prevailed.

Consider this as one small example of the contradictions we face in navigating the modern media: a left, very popular critic of US capitalism, published by a giant firm based in New York, in turn only one arm of a truly global media empire – the News Corporation – owned by a right-wing Australian; a local group trying to publish and disseminate left/feminist ideas and hoping to increase their profile by snagging a US celebrity too busy on the fast track to notice. *Stupid White Men* is a good political book and we should all feel encouraged that Michael Moore's message is getting heard. The book remains high on the best-seller lists. HarperCollins keeps reprinting and generating very healthy returns. Maybe sometime soon they'll bring out a paperback version under $20.

And Matt is still searching for Michael Moore's home email.

Media saturation

In almost every corner of the globe – in London and Lagos, Beijing and Boulogne, Delhi and Tuba City – the media shape the way most of us live our lives. Media content floods in and swirls around us, affecting the way we think and act and dream. For others, in poorer or remoter parts of the world, the saturation may be less intense but the influence can still be considerable.

Despite huge differences in distance, upbringing and social context, many of us now listen to the same music, read the same books and watch the same films and television. Youth in Soweto listen to LA rap; viewers in southern China's Guangdong province watch pirated tapes of Jackie Chan; Sri Lankan refugee kids in Toronto come home from school to settle down in front of Tamil movies rented from the local grocery store. Teenagers and their young siblings in almost every place on earth know Bart and Lisa Simpson. I can sit at my home computer downloading the latest communiqués from Mexico's indigenous Zapatista rebels and out of the corner of my eye watch the World Cup live from Korea on the TV in the next room.

Much of this global sharing is not, of course, entirely new. International exchange of culture and ideas through the mass media has been commonplace for a

The media – a modern concept

Contemporary use of the word media still carries a trace of its original Latin meaning of 'medium' or 'middle'. The singular noun, medium, is a link or intermediate agent between places or things, thus a medium in chemistry holds particles together, or a medium can be a device of transport for reaching another place. A dog-sled is a 'medium' of transport. So, in the 18th century newspapers began to be called a medium for ideas and advertising. Collectively they became news media. By the 20th century, with the coming of radio and television and the large companies or government departments that manage them, the new plural sense of the word began to be used.

Thus we now refer to 'the media' as entities unto themselves (or even one homogenous thing). In this sense media no longer act simply as devices or neutral carriers of ideas, but are the source of those ideas and meanings. They are a central element of power, with structures and rules and conventions unto themselves. It's in this sense that Marshall McLuhan's glib phrase, 'The Medium is the Message', rings true.

Today, the media include newspapers, cinema, radio and recording, television and the internet. Throughout this book I'll refer to specific media but it is useful to think of several characteristics that they hold in common. They are:

- producers and distributors of news, entertainment and information
- engaged in the handling of sophisticated technology of recording, distribution and reception
- distributed to very large and socially diverse audiences whose individual members are usually unknown to each other – in this sense they are 'mass' media
- institutions – not simple companies or government agencies but complex organizations with symbolic functions
- theoretically accessible to all (there is nothing in the science or technology itself that is designed for some specific group in society – they function primarily as broadcasters)
- powerful forces of capitalism in most societies – in economic terms they are hugely wealthy and wield political as well as cultural and ideological power ■

century. But perhaps the speed, indeed the simultaneity and the increasing flow add up to something new. The time seems right to speak of *world* media.

The concept of media is now also used in the technical/political sense, but without any mass or institutional elements. Hence we hear terms such as 'media activists' and the 'independent media', to describe political artists using a semi-professional digital camera or low power radio to document or comment on events. Thus the general term, media activist, has begun to take over from 'filmmaker', 'photographer', even 'video activist'. This usage seems to be based on both the fact that audio-visual technologies are digital and to signal an oppositional stance toward the dominant media conceived as a single entity.

In trying to deal with the scope and diversity of the media some writers concentrate on the *news* media. Others stick to entertainment. My approach here will be to treat both news and entertainment together and throughout the book show why this combined analysis makes sense.

Globalization

Globalization carries many useful yet also contradictory meanings. As a description of today's world, interconnected more than ever before through technology and science (two fields that will concern us in detail later in the book), the term globalization certainly makes sense. It can also be very useful in describing the state of contemporary economics, politics and culture. In some fields of endeavor we now have, or are moving toward, broad structures, practices and policies that organize the world as a whole and shape our view of how we might live in it. Three of the most obvious examples are the world financial markets, the United Nations and the internet. But globalization is patchier and less universal than we are sometimes led to believe. As Eric Hobsbawm argues: 'Politically speaking, we have a world that remains in reality pluralist and divided into territorial states. In the current situation, there is... a coexistence of two different systems; one for the economy and one for politics.'[1] Thus, throughout the book I will emphasize three movements or trends: those pushing toward globalization; those elements that complicate or constrain that trend; and those movements toward diversity or pluralism. Because the media comprise technology, politics, economics, culture and art, globalization will not suffice as an all-encompassing term.

I began with the statement that the media shape our lives. Now, I need to complicate that idea and add two other realities. First, our outlook and ways of living get shaped by many factors other than the media, primarily the face-to-face relations of work, school, family and neighborhood. These relations can be lived and felt completely apart from the media. Clifford Stoll, one of the earliest skeptics of internet hype reminds us in his 1995 book *Silicon Snake Oil* that 'few aspects of daily life require computers... They're irrelevant to cooking, driving, visiting, negotiating, eating, hiking, dancing, speaking and gossiping.'[2]

The problem is that it remains difficult to sort out *how* we are influenced – do we react to each other simply as humans or do our media-influenced manners, dress and even speech play a role as well? Is our first youthful kiss purely the result of hormonal urges and attraction, or is it also modeled on the way we've seen it performed thousands of times in the movies? Do we hold off kissing at all because the films we watch never show it, as is the case in conventional Indian film? This question of influence can also be deadly serious: the 1994 genocide in Rwanda of the Tutsi minority and Hutu dissenters was facilitated by a concerted, vicious hate campaign carried out on the official state radio.

One group that certainly believes we can be strongly influenced by the media are advertisers. Television advertising works especially hard to link objects and services that are for sale with ideas prevalent in our culture. The ads didn't create these ideas; in fact it is because the ideas carry the legitimacy of real life, lived apart from media, that they often work so well. 'All ads contain the fundamental meaning, "Buy this product,"' says television theorist Jeremy Butler, 'but they also suggest various other meanings that range from "Buy this product *and* you will become beautiful," to "Buy this product *and* you will be well liked" to "Buy this product *and* your dog's fur will really shine."' Butler shows that television commercials present an ongoing discourse about objects and attempt to connect them to a range of meanings. He identifies eight categories of meanings:

1. Luxury, leisure and conspicuous consumption
2. Individualism
3. The natural
4. Folk culture and tradition
5. Novelty and progress
6. Sexuality and romance
7. Alleviation of pain, fear/anxiety and guilt
8. Utopia and escape from dystopia[3]

Again, all of these meanings can have validity quite apart from media. To reiterate, the problem of unraveling how, and to what extent, we are shaped by media is a complex one. I will return to these ideas of media influence and media and society later in the book.

The second point to remember is that we experience the media differently across the world. Not only are we influenced in complex ways but we are shaped differently depending on our place in the world and our exposure to various media forms. Here in the West, media saturation pours into every nook of our lives. Todd Gitlin, author of *Media Unlimited* believes that the 'super-saturation' of media in the US has profoundly changed the American psyche. It has grown all-pervasive, ever colonizing more of our space and time. Although we can 'navigate' our immediate exposure within media culture by adopting various personae – the fan, the secessionist, the content critic – the polluting effects spread like crop spray on the wind, says Gitlin. There seems no escape: 'Unless we click an off button or smash the screen, the images stream on... They are with us even if we are not with them.'[4]

Elsewhere, half the world's population has never made a phone call. In many countries illiteracy remains stubbornly high, particularly for girls and women. In other places the rigid state control of news and much entertainment leaves readers, listeners and viewers to think of media as something distant and imposed and therefore of no value in their immediate lives.

Even with a program that it almost universally watched, the experience can vary enormously. In South Korea, *The Simpsons* draws millions of viewers for its quirky voices and the vaguely familiar family dynamics (dads can be buffoons anywhere), an enjoyable product of commercial culture beamed in by Star TV's satellite. Perhaps some Korean viewers even know the women who draw the animation panels, farmed out by the show to Asia to cut costs. In the US the show forms part of the national fabric, simply 'American', hardly the commercial product of Rupert Murdoch's Fox TV network. In some households around the world the show comes across as a brilliant satire on the stupidities of US life. Elsewhere, it is read as rather harmless, conveying a fun patina of family-values. And at Queens' College, Cambridge University, every Sunday night the grad students gather faithfully to watch Homer and kin. It is entirely possible that when they miss a question in class next day they exclaim, 'D'oh!'

Where broadcast TV, cable and theatrical cinema offer limited fare, audiences adapt. Thus, in Saudi Arabia 85 per cent of households owned a VCR by 1985. In Brazil, a country mad about its TV serial melodramas, or *telenovelas*, distributed via the free terrestrial networks, cable and satellite also provide international programming choice, but only for the wealthy. In the poorest countries of the world, such as

Mozambique and Malawi, any TV remains beyond reach for most people and thus radio plays a key role – and often the languages of broadcast reach only the Portuguese- and English-speaking minorities.

World media often appear to flow freely, the result of universal popularity and ever-cheaper technologies such as cassettes, videotape, telephone and internet connections and widely diffused paper books. Even higher priced cinema tickets and personal computers seem within range of the working and middle classes everywhere. If we look at the specifics, however, we can see numerous patterns of exchange and flow. I will begin by outlining three different sorts of international relationships involving media: a diffusion of dominant media, encounters and cross-pollination.

Dominant diffusion: cultural imperialism

Most audiences rarely think of the mass media, particularly cinema, television and recorded music as purely commercial products. Since the 1950s these are predominantly US products. From *I Love Lucy* to Madonna, the accents and manners often carry very specific reference points: Beverly Hills 90201, Beale Street, State Street, Sunset Strip; *Sleepless in Seattle, Chicago Hope, LA Law;* FBI, FDA, INS, CIA.

In the past, most nation states with world pretensions used a combination of raw force, commercial clout and a hearts-and-minds cultural campaign to establish imperial rule. Throughout the 19th century the French and British were particularly adept and, as Edward Said wrote in his classic studies *Culture and Imperialism* and *Orientalism,* the entire world became

---

Action for export

'Everyone understands an action movie. If I tell you a joke, you may not get it but if a bullet goes through the window we all know to hit the floor, no matter what the language.' ■

Larry Gordon, producer of *Die Hard, Die Hard 2.5*

divided into spheres of us and them, civil and uncivil, Occidental and Oriental. For the past century US political and economic influence has been aided immensely by US film and music. Where the marines, missionaries and bureaucrats failed, Charlie Chaplin, Mickey Mouse and The Beach Boys have succeeded effortlessly in attracting the world to the American way. Simultaneously, the US State Department has played a key role in facilitating the flow of US cultural products across the world. According to the Motion Picture Association of America Hollywood films and TV take in $32 billion annually. Unlike the US economy as a whole, now burdened with a $400 billion annual trade deficit, Hollywood, alone among US business enterprises, boasts a surplus balance of trade.[6]

In tandem with equally prominent brands, such as McDonalds and NIKE, Disney products are impossible to avoid in any major city of the world. It's this

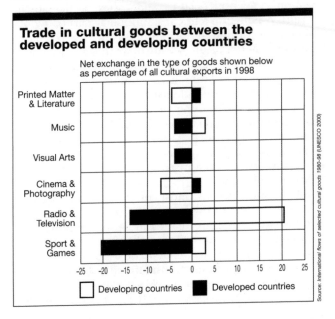

Trade in cultural goods between the developed and developing countries

Net exchange in the type of goods shown below as percentage of all cultural exports in 1998

Printed Matter & Literature

Music

Visual Arts

Cinema & Photography

Radio & Television

Sport & Games

-25 -20 -15 -10 -5 0 5 10 15 20 25

☐ Developing countries   ■ Developed countries

Source: International flows of selected cultural goods 1980-98 (UNESCO 2000)

never-ending flow of McWorld values and products that makes a concept like cultural imperialism so compelling.

Yet, the theories of cultural and media imperialism have also been criticized on both empirical and analytic grounds. Some scholars feel that these theories tend to see the world in terms of center and periphery, with the Third World as unitary and comprised only of victims or dupes. A look at contemporary India, for example, reveals a complex society that hardly fits the unitary mold. Ramaswami Harindraneth writes about three new phenomena shaping modern India: the rise of religious fundamentalism; the growth of opposition social movements, opposed, for example, to the Narmada Dam project; and the 'much celebrated' software industry – the 'Silicon Valley of Bangalore'.[7] These contradictory trends highlight the difficulty of applying simplified notions of imperialism or globalization. The upper-classes and castes participate in wealth production and consumption as part of a global elite. According to Harindraneth and others a more accurate model of the world shows that each country or region of the globe experiences a polarization of local populations into haves and have-nots. Rather than one dominant cultural force, situated as in the past in Western Europe or the US, several regional centers now struggle for media and cultural power. As one writer describes it, world television flows are extremely complex, 'a patchwork quilt rather than a one-way street' comprised of 'intricate and multi-directional flows'.[8]

The situation in most of South and Central America confirms this concept of regional power and shows the strength of 'Latin' programming and indigenous control of the media. Two companies in particular, *Televisa* in Mexico and *Globo* of Brazil are themselves significant transnationals, second in size and scope only to the world's largest broadcasters. Both *Televisa* and *Globo* not only dominate TV in their home countries but export significant amounts of programming within the Americas and to Europe. The 250 million Spanish and 175 million Portuguese speakers throughout the world guarantee a huge market, starved for new media forms in their own language. Thus, according to the critics of the cultural imperialism model, the empirical realities of transnational trade, whether we call it globalization or not, show that Western media imperialism no longer applies. Australian media theorist John Sinclair argues that we need to move away from the dominant 'West versus passive Third World' model and develop what he terms 'middle-level analysis', such as an examination of regional distribution and production. For Sinclair, although the US commercial model of media is now dominant, it no longer needs US products to develop.

But, as useful as a middle-level analysis can be, Sinclair and others surely exaggerate the demise of Western media as agents of meanings and power across the globe. The reality is that US cultural imperialism is far from exhausted. Rupert Murdoch may feel no loyalty to Australia or his adopted US, but his Fox TV and competitor Disney are built on Americana. EuroDisney can serve crêpes at its French theme park but Mickey and Uncle Sam still walk arm in arm.

Encounters

Without doubt the media enable myriad encounters of ideas, artistic expressions and cultural meanings. These encounters can be the result of cultural flows in many directions – not only North to South but also from the so-called periphery to the metropolitan centers and within regions of the South. At the turn of the 20th century, French cinema dominated screens around the world, starting with the Lumière family's proto-documentaries or *actualities*. As the Lumière camera operators traveled, filming and projecting with their sixteen-pound *cinématographes*, audiences everywhere were entranced to see not only Paris and Lyon but contemporary scenes from Russia, Algeria, China, Peru – in fact nearly every region of the world. The fascination with European cinema continued throughout the century that brought us Renoir and Visconti, Bergman, Bardot and Godard. In those same years of the early 20th century gramophone recordings such as Emile Berliner's Bluebird disks, produced in Montreal, gave listeners a taste of European concert standards. The encounter was felt not only in the homes of the wealthy but also by working people and the poor within the public sphere.

Other types of encounter are characterized by respect where occasional elements of style, theme, or performance get incorporated into the other culture. But for the most part these styles remain exotic or minority tastes. Today, for example, small African musical groups mixing popular and traditional styles, such as the Orchestra Baobab of Senegal, get noticed, recorded and promoted widely in Europe and North America.

Another fascinating encounter involves the popularity of Brazilian *telenovelas* not only in South America but in China, Indonesia and post-Soviet Russia, where accounts report that the streets empty when the program comes on. John Sinclair writes: 'This success suggests more universal qualities which quite diverse audiences find in *telenovelas*, perhaps due to their intrinsic temporal rhythms or allegorical character, perhaps the result of *Globo*'s experience in the cultivation of audience appeal across regional and other differences within Brazil.'[8]

Cross-pollination

In addition to a simple encounter and appreciation for the previously unknown, foreign and exotic, all sorts of genuine and lasting influence can also take place. For some musicians, in Paris and London, for example, contemporary West African styles of performance and orchestration make such an impression as to create an almost immediate shift and an attempt to incorporate. Thus the African style affects and changes other music or performance. Something new can flower. Audiences might take to the hybrid or be encouraged to follow the trail back to the original.

In cinema, anyone who has seen the original 1970s martial arts films of Sammo Hung or Bruce Lee knows the incredible influence of that form of stylized choreography on action cinema the world over. Another key Hong Kong director, Ringo Lam, director of *City on Fire, Full Contact* and others has traveled in both directions: born in Hong Kong, he studied film at York University in Toronto, returned to enormous success in Hong Kong during the 1980s and on to Hollywood in the late 1990s. US jazz with its roots in African and European forms has not only doubled back to Africa but mixed with many Southern currents – notably the so-called Latin forms from Brazil, Cuba and Haiti. These are much more than simple encounters. They have led to wholly new sounds – perhaps a world music – which stir new musical feelings and emotions. With cross-pollination musicians start to write and perform in new ways.

This cross-pollination or hybrid-making can be *alternative* to mainstream forms, as in many types of world music or *oppositional* in social as well as cultural terms. As corporations become transnational and wars displace millions, creating migrants, refugees and diasporic communities, many media makers try to respond and fight the worst elements of commercial culture and murderous nationalism.

Becoming digital: new information and communication technologies

A newer and slightly different approach to media study centers on the information and communication technologies (ICT) that make mass media possible. Since the 1980s the idea of convergence has seemed pertinent because the digital science of computers underlies or strongly shapes the entire range of media. The seductive notion of technological change and converging media has reached mantra status.

Even the 'old' media of newspapers, film and radio have integrated digital technology into design, production and distribution. Digital processes now affect the design of newspapers and books; control the application of color in film, video and printing inks; provide the basis for radio recording and satellite transmission; and in cinema hasten the shift to digital photography and editing. The 'new' media of CDs and web pages are new precisely because they are possible only through computers.

Hybrid beats: Orchestra Baobab

In the 1970s Senegal's dance music scene was ruled by Orchestra Baobab, a multi-ethnic, multi-national group strongly influenced by post-second world war Cuban dance styles such as calypso and salsa and by Latin love songs. They called their style variété or 'salad'. The band featured seven seasoned performers led by larger-than-life Dakar native Issa Cissoko on sax, who comes from a Malian musical family, and Barthelemy Attisso on Les Paul guitar from Togo. Vocals were supplied by Rudy Gomas from Guinea Bissau. Baobab's music reflected the philosophy of negritude championed by the country's first President, Leopold Senghor: 'It had to be modern – to suit the mood of independence – and rooted in local traditions.'

By the early 1980s Senegal was engulfed in political turmoil and the eclectic music of the streets was sparking new influences – new Muslim rhythms, traditional drum styles and US hip-hop. The teenage Youssou N'Dour captured and blended these varied strands into a new mix he called mblalax and became West Africa's first superstar of World Music. The world seemed to have passed Baobab by. They retired, Cuban music went out of style, and Attisso returned to Togo to become a lawyer.

But the trans-Atlantic flows between West Africa and the Caribbean never stop. As elsewhere around the globe, the phenomenal success of The Buena Vista Social Club recordings and film in the late 1990s revived the Cuban influence. An opportunity appeared. It was seized on by a leading producer at World Circuit Records in Britain, Nick Gold, who had co-produced the Buena Vista recordings. Gold convinced the musicians to regroup and the new Orchestra Baobab was born. With

This ICT approach usually includes discussion of the huge and growing field of data processing, or information technologies – from DNA mapping and medical information, to weather reports, satellite surveillance, census and other public and private statistics and the flow of information on the internet. Through this approach comes the seductive but absolutely vague idea that we now live in the Information Age. But technological change and corporate growth are blurring the boundaries between news, entertainment and supposedly neutral information. Hence the birth of computer-television hybrid MSNBC and the move by the publishing giant International Thomson to abandon newspapers and books for the business of

---

the help of N'Dour and his Senegal-based record label and significantly the world distribution backing of Nonesuch, a subsidiary of Warner Music, a new album, Specialists in All Styles soon followed. To push the world music marketing, both N'Dour and Ibrahim Ferrer, the star of Buena Vista were brought in to sing backup. Orchestra Baobab immediately took off on tour to Europe.

The Orchestra Baobab salad:

- traditional West African djembe drums
- French colonial dance music influenced by Cuban calypso and salsa, plus Latin love songs
- various strands of Dakar and regional musics
- a new, younger audience of Senegalese youth weaned on hip-hop
- a Togo guitarist, on vacation from his law practice, who lists his influences as Dr Nico of Congo and BB King
- British world music producers
- references of style and sensibility to other world music icons Youssou N'Dour and Ibrahim Ferrer
- a 'post-modern' jokey consciousness that boasts of being 'specialists in all styles' signaling a sophisticated wink and a warning to its audience not to 'take any one strand of the music as a pure and simple essence'

The media culture of world music (seen by music companies as a new brand) thus defies easy generalizations with a mixed salad of this complexity. Equal doses of West African traditional and Warner's transnational clout propel the Baobab's new sound to open and curious listeners everywhere. ■

Source: Nick Gold, 'Orchestra Baobab biography', www.orchestrabaobab.com

data and on-line information products. But this tech-
nology-focused approach tends to shift the attention
from those aspects of politics and the corporate economy that control the pace and adoption of technology.
For example, in the 1920s the US recording industry
switched to electric recording, a technology that had
been around for years. The impetus was the new competition with commercial radio.[9]

Human rights

The 50 years since the Second World War have seen
the gradual development of wide-ranging legislation
and agreements concerning trade as well as international human and cultural rights. Both local and
international media play a key role in promoting or
hindering this process. For example, since the 1960s
many furious disputes have erupted at the United
Nations and the World Trade Organization over 'global media' and 'local culture'. These have increasingly
eclipsed more traditional economic struggles over
agriculture, science and the law of the sea. French /
US hostility was recently most intense over Iraq, however the French defense of their 'cultural heritage' at
the World Trade Organization (WTO) has for many
years carried a specific anti-US charge.

At the UN the 1948 Universal Declaration of
Human Rights contained a number of clauses that
have been used as ammunition in these disputes.
Article 19 of the Declaration appears to take cultural
rights beyond the passive right to read and watch and
states that every person has the 'right to receive **and
impart** information and ideas through any media'.
This might be summarized as the 'right to communicate and to be an active producer of ideas'.[10] These
cultural rights became more concrete in the 1966
International Covenant on Economic, Social and
Cultural Rights. Article 15 of the Covenant states that
everyone has the right to 'take part in cultural life,'
and that governments, 'must be active in encouraging

and promoting culture'. Cambridge University legal scholar Roger O'Keefe has documented how Article 15 has evolved.[11] From the original, rather high-brow, concern to make great works of art accessible to the masses, the committee has taken up popular culture, newspapers and magazines and most recently the communications media. In case national governments treat this as merely an abstract declaration, in 1976 a strenuous monitoring committee was established. In addition, governments have been 'expected to take reactive measures against overly aggressive foreign cultural influences,' states O'Keefe. Article 15 insists that governments not only try to limit cultural discrimination, they must also take active measures to broaden cultural access. For example, the Committee has specifically warned various governments to 'keep a watch on satellite and cable TV operations'. In the case of Jordan, says O'Keefe, the Committee questioned the powerful role of satellite and cable TV, yet 'appeared unperturbed that the Libyan authorities permitted the installation and use of satellite dishes'. This, according to O'Keefe, is not inconsistency but a recognition that a diversity of cultures can only be maintained by a diversity of means. His study concludes that the Committee has 'adroitly balanced the right to enjoy a distinctive national culture with the competing demands for the freedom to receive outside cultural input'.

During the 1990s the action on culture and commerce shifted to the World Trade Organization. Under the banner of neoliberal globalization, all goods and services should be allowed to travel freely without restrictions and the 'WTO is generally more favorable to the trading interests of the major industrial countries,' says Cees Hamelink.[12] He goes on: 'In its basic mandate the WTO violates the core of the human rights system: the recognition that all people should be treated equitably'. For the US, these goods and services clearly include film, television, music

'The Globalizer' – Rupert Murdoch

Rupert Murdoch may be the most powerful media person on the planet. If there is a role model for executives who aspire to global business, and a target for those who detest the commercial ethos of transnational media, it is Murdoch and his News Corporation. The strength of his empire flows from his strong positions in developing both content and distribution while maintaining family control of the firm.

In 1952 Murdoch got off to a running start – he inherited *The Adelaide News* from his father Sir Keith Murdoch. Today his reach is awesome. Here is a partial list.

Britain:
- BSkyB – Europe's most successful satellite television system
- The Times newspaper and The News of the World

US:
- Twentieth Century Fox film studios
- Fox TV network – producer of The X-Files and The Simpsons
- *The New York Post*
- TV Guide

Asia:
- Hong Kong's Star TV
- China – Star and Phoenix TV and a 2003 partnership with the state-owned Guangdong TV network
- Australia – more than 50 per cent of all newspapers sold
- India – Star brands plus Vijay, broadcasting to South India's Tamil population

News Corporation owns HarperCollins, one of the largest publishers in the world and publishes more than 174 newspapers, employing 115,000 people and printing more than 40 million papers a week.

Murdoch's presence today is felt most keenly in Britain for his

recordings, books, magazines and computer software. After all, these comprise five per cent of the US economy – more than US agriculture or steel production. For the rest of the world, which can feel as though it is drowning in US culture, the need to create protections for domestic production and to exempt culture from trade liberalization seems crucial.

In the past and continuing today, countries that worried about US film, TV and music tried various methods of stemming the flow or altering the power dynamic. These countries covered the political spectrum, from social-democratic France to Islamic Iran and Brazil's notorious military dictatorship of the

ownership of both ends of the newspaper market's 'taste spectrum', his mailed-fist lobbying to scrap the Government's foreign media and cross-media ownership rules and perhaps above all, in elite circles, the way he forced the BBC out of China in 1994 by blocking access to his satellite. In the US Murdoch's Fox TV is targeted by social conservatives as the harbinger of new lows in trash. At the same time, neoliberal defenders of commercial media, including Michael Powell, head of the Federal Communication Commission, point to Fox as proof that the US system is dynamic, open to newcomers and constantly expanding in order to give consumers more choice.

In 2002 Murdoch named his son Lachlan as publisher of *The New York Post* followed by the 2003 appointment of his youngest, 30-year-old James, as non-executive director of BSkyB. So the family dynasty rolls on.

A 2003 survey by *The Guardian* newspaper of Murdoch's 175 editors world-wide, headlined 'Their Master's Voice', showed 'an extraordinary unity of thought' on going to war with Iraq. Media columnist Roy Greenslade wrote, 'You have got to admit that Rupert Murdoch is one canny press tycoon because he has an unerring ability to choose editors across the world who think just like him. How else can we explain the extraordinary unity of thought in his newspaper empire about the need to make war on Iraq? It is clear that [all his editors] are singing from the same hymn sheet. Some are bellicose baritone soloists who relish the fight. Some prefer a less strident, if more subtle, role in the chorus. But none, whether fortissimo or pianissimo, has dared to croon the anti-war tune. Their master's voice has never been questioned.' ∎

Source: Roy Greenslade, 'Their Master's Voice', in *The Guardian*, 17 February 2003.

1960s and 70s. They attempted either restrictive strategies or the stimulus approach, and sometimes both at once. Restrictions have included attempts to block US products through taxes and tariffs; prohibitions on foreign ownership; labor laws; and quotas, for example on the percentage of foreign films screened. Other methods of stimulus include support for local culture through tax breaks, subsidies and incentives to production or distribution, aid to artists and producers, development of technical infrastructures such as microwave and satellite and the creation of training or scholarship programs. Some of these methods have been effective, at least for a time. However, many of

GATS attack

What is GATS?

The General Agreement on Trade in Services (GATS) is an international trade agreement that came into effect in 1995 and operates under the umbrella of the World Trade Organization (WTO). The aim of the GATS is to gradually remove all barriers to trade in services.

Services can be explained as anything that you cannot drop on your foot! Our libraries, schools, hospitals, banks, rubbish collection and even the water that we clean our teeth with are all services that feed our daily lives. And it includes almost all cultural industries under its broad terms.

A growing number of local and national governments, trade unions, NGOs and political activists of all sorts are calling for a halt on the negotiations. Their main points of critique include:

- Negative effects on universal access to basic services such as healthcare, education, water and public service broadcasting.
- Fundamental conflict between freeing up trade in services and the right of governments and communities to regulate companies in areas such as tourism, retail, telecommunications and broadcasting, eg countries will be unable to restrict majority foreign ownership of domestic media.
- A one-sided deal: GATS is primarily about expanding opportunities for large multinational companies.

It elevates trade rules above all other values in the cultural and media sectors. The world's most powerful banks, media corporations and Western governments could use the GATS process to undercut the principles of universal cultural rights embodied in the 1948 and 1966 Human Rights agreements. ∎

Sources:
GATSwatch www.gatswatch.org, based in The Netherlands
World Development Movement www.wdm.org, based in the UK
The Council of Canadians www.canadians.org, based in Canada.
Public Citizen www.citizen.org, based in the US.

these strategies now face stiff challenges in trade negotiations or behind the scenes arm-twisting.

A much more ambitious scheme of the 1960s and 70s, this time on a global scale, attempted to address what many southern analysts saw as the one-way flow of news and entertainment from the North to the South. This famous initiative, organized by UNESCO and known as the New World Information and Communication Order (NWICO), gained considerable momentum among the Non-Aligned countries of the South and ferocious opposition from the US, which eventually stopped it dead.

Ironically, it is the US that plays the restrictive game best. Only a minuscule number of foreign films – less than one per cent – play on US screens, down from ten per cent available to viewers in the 1970s. The US government supports its film and television industries through tax breaks and dozens of indirect subsidies to states and local municipalities and it restricts foreign ownership of newspapers and television stations. A recent and highly controversial form of support involves the handovers of digital radio licenses and the internet infrastructure to private interests. The US media lobby has successfully hidden this massive aid, hypocritically denouncing other countries for subsidizing their art and cultural industries.[13] In fact, as media critic Robert McChesney argues, the entire fabric of the US media system is the result of a series of political decisions. This started with the fundamental decisions early in the 20th century to make radio and TV broadcasting commercial, rather than public entities. At the WTO and elsewhere US negotiators argue that other countries unfairly restrict US culture and, as US commercial firms, they shouldn't have to 'bear the brunt of the financial costs associated with achieving [other people's] cultural policy objectives'.[14]

Here again, however, the dynamic between US interests and transnational capital is shifting. Three examples: Sony Corporation owns Columbia Pictures; VNU (United Dutch Publishers) owns the ACNielsen media polling company; and perhaps most embarrassing of all for US nationalists, Vivendi of France owns a piece of Universal Studios.

The time has come to take an international approach to the media. This is because as viewers, readers and listeners, even in different parts of the world, we have much in common. Also, according to advocates of globalization theory (whether they view it as positive or negative) media companies now operate beyond the national boundaries of their head office or

place of origin. In addition, incredible developments
in technology have led to a continuing shrinkage of
time and space – satellite broadcast and the instant
communication of the internet comprising the clearest examples. Yet despite common media experiences
and a shrinking world simple notions of globalization
and cultural imperialism will not suffice – some elements of technology, science and economics are
leading to universal (global) standards and practices,
yet politics and culture remain stubbornly local, fractured and diverse.

The modern media have developed into industries
like no other, partly because their power stems from
various portions of political and commercial decision
making. In order to understand in more detail the various ways that politics and economics mix the next
chapter will outline a political economy approach to
the media.

1 *The New Century*, Eric Hobsbawm (The New Press 2000). **2** Clifford Stoll,
Silicon Snake Oil: Second Thoughts on the Information Highway (Anchor
1995). **3** Jeremy Butler, *Television: Critical Methods and Applications*
(Lawrence Erlbaum Associates 2002). **4** Todd Gitlin, *Media Unlimited: How
the Torrent of Images and Sounds Overwhelms Our Lives* (Henry Holt 2001).
5 Quoted in Ken Auletta, *The Highwaymen* (Random House 1997). **6** Jack
Valenti, Motion Picture Association of America press release, 25 September
2002. **7** Ramaswami Harindraneth, 'Software Industry, Religious
Nationalism and Social Movements in India: Aspects of Globalization?', in
Manjunath Pendakur and Roma Harris, *Citizenship and Participation in the
Information Age* (Garamond Press 2002). **8** John Sinclair et al, *New Patterns
in Global Television: Peripheral Vision* (Oxford 1996). **9** Brian Winston,
*Media, Technology and Society: A History: From the Telegraph to the
Internet* (Routledge 1998). **10** William F Birdsall and Merrilee Rasmussen,
'The Citizen's Right to Communicate', in Pendakur and Harris, op. cit.
11 Roger O'Keefe, 'The "Right to take part in cultural life" under Article 15
of the ICESVR', in *International and Comparative Law Quarterly*, October
1998. **12** Cees Hamelink, 'Human Rights in the Information Society', in
Pendakur and Harris, op. cit. **13** Robert McChesney, *Rich Media, Poor
Democracy: Communications Politics in Dubious Times*, (The New Press
2001). **14** William S Merkin, US trade negotiator, President and CEO,
Strategic Policy Inc., quoted in Elie Cohen, 'Globalization and cultural diversity,' in UNESCO, *World Culture Report 2000, Cultural diversity, conflict and
pluralism* (UNESCO 2000).

3 Political economy: the howling, brawling, global marketplace

The dominant media have the power to set political agendas and shape the cultural landscape. The media companies play important economic and symbolic roles in most modern states. But although these 'cultural industries' have grown to immense size and their power has become ever more concentrated they are not omnipotent. Many contradictions and conflicts within the companies and between companies and states allow for initiatives toward democratic media.

Defining dominant media

SOMETIMES IN EVERYDAY conversation we refer to the industries of film, television and radio simply as the mass media. After all, most media production takes shape on a large scale, similar to the mass production of other products such as steel, autos and toasters, and because the media reach a huge market for their products. In addition, this huge market for media forms includes a diverse range of people from most social and economic groups – a mass audience rather than a smaller, specialized segment.

But two problems arise with the term 'mass media'. First, if we consider the media as modes of economic production, 'mass' seems too neutral a term, too detached from the active power that media wield in shaping ideas and creating meanings. Second, if we consider media in terms of cultural activity, the term 'mass media' implies a homogenous audience that will receive, consume, be affected by, or use the product or service in a uniform way. This notion of mass production for a mass audience is often accompanied by elitist connotations that mass means cheap and unrefined.

Thus, the term 'mass media' fails to describe the ability of media to control and shape the direction of society, the range of content quality and the diversity of audiences.

Another shorthand term you often hear is 'mainstream media'. But this refers primarily to the cultural rather than the economic elements and again overlooks the ability of big media to limit diversity, to control key economic factors and to shape political agendas.

The concept of 'dominant media' avoids these problems and reminds us of the power to influence and power to exclude other voices. It reminds us that the media function in ways that are both political as well as economic.

Dominant media take different forms in various countries and within different media sectors, along a spectrum that ranges from totally state controlled to almost entirely left to the market. In the US, the big firms operate within a commercial model and the government regulations work primarily to facilitate stable economic conditions. US TV has national networks but the newspapers – save the skimpy *USA Today* – are

---

Shock-jocks and gatekeepers: US radio

In 1996 a series of deals and acquisitions began to change the face of US pop radio. Now, one company, Clear Channel Communications, run by Randy Michaels, a former shock-jock DJ akin to the ultra right-wing Howard Stern, has emerged as the nation's largest radio broadcaster. It owns 1,225 stations. Prior to 1996 the US government restricted radio corporations from controlling too many stations. Companies could own only two in any one market and no more than 28 nationwide. The rules were designed to keep ownership as diverse as possible and to encourage a local focus. Clear Channel's lightning fast acquisitions spree gives it prominence in the nation's 250 top radio markets, especially for Top 40 and rock-radio. This provides one of the clearest examples of recent media concentration, placing a small number of people in charge of choosing what listeners will hear. ■

Eric Broelert, 'Record Companies: Save us from ourselves', in *Salon*, 13 March 2002.

regional. In Britain, France, Canada and Japan, the state has traditionally played a stronger role and insisted on additional principles of public service. Brazil's *Globo* TV rose to prominence simultaneously with the military dictatorship (1964-1985) and now operates unchecked as a commercial enterprise, in a national situation best referred to as 'maverick capitalism' and with no real attending notions of public service. Mexico's *Televisa* has been closely connected to the authoritarian, one-party rule of the PRI (Institutional Revolutionary Party) which ended only in 2000. In Korea three private groups – *Chosun Ilbo, JoonAng Ilbo and Dong-A Ilbo* – dominate the press. These rose to power in the 1980s when Korea's military government ceded media control to the private sector. In China, dominant media is aligned with the Communist Party. Although commercial criteria are pushing to the fore, particularly in the realm of satellite TV, these have not yet achieved much independence from the goals of the Party media.

In India, the constellation of dominant media organizations imposes Hindu language and culture, and even that of a standardized sort. The long-established state broadcaster, Doordarshan, say researchers Manas Ray and Elizabeth Jacka, 'reproduces a select set of language, religion and regions in attempting to produce an unequivocal, homogenous national image.'[1] India's population of one billion speaks 16 regional languages and 800 dialects. However, Hindi and English prevail as the official languages despite being spoken by only 40 per cent of the population. Thus, in India dominant media have a key role in building a unified state identity. Even after major changes in the 1990s that brought satellite, cable and private broadcasting, Doordarshan remains the only network allowed to transmit terrestrially or to provide satellite uplinks from within the country. This makes it difficult for the private networks or foreign interests to offer a news service.

As I suggested in Chapter Two, many people now refer to the media as a single entity, a power unto itself, akin to the church, the family and the school system as a key institution comprising the fabric of society. Certainly, in thinking about the contemporary international media some kinds of generalizations make sense. Yet, the older (still grammatically correct) sense of the media, which always speaks in the plural, of newspapers, the film industry, radio, publishing and so forth, should not be lost. This is because each media sector operates according to specific conditions, traditions, practices and rules – true even for media operations within a transnational conglomerate. In this sense Bertelsmann's German magazine empire runs quite differently from their Random House subsidiary in New York. Time Warner manages CNN in a wholly different context than its record division. In the global film business Hollywood still completely dominates (except for India) in terms of exports and revenues. But nowhere does it control the cultural or political agenda of any specific country. So, for example, in studying how the dominant media function in Mexico we would need to consider Hollywood films, *Televisa* TV and the purely national and regional print media, aligned to one or other of the three political parties. In a similar fashion, the top five recording companies Universal, Warners, BMG, Sony and EMI far outpace others in sales but do not dominate commercial radio outside the US.

'Dominant' increasingly refers to the global arena. Here we return to the debates over the power of the transnationals. This is where the distinction between <u>scale</u> of operations and domination proves useful. To return to the case of Rupert Murdoch's News Corp, aside from his newspaper supremacy across Australia, in no other country do his papers or television operations completely dominate. Nevertheless, in terms of overall global power News Corp has attained immense influence. Its Sky and Star satellite operations in particular pose a serious challenge to national broadcasters on every continent. Even the mere threat of a Murdoch invasion has forced many countries to make changes in media legislation. Another contender for world domination is the Disney Corporation, which since the 1930s has exerted immense influence in promoting the US brand of cultural and economic life. Again, although not dominant in any single country the Disney brands can be found nearly everywhere and their influence over children's media and culture cannot be overstated. Thus, in thinking about dominant media it is important to consider not only size alone but international reach, and not only news or editorial content but also cultural and political influence.

Concentration of ownership

In market economies most industries operate best when a variety of companies engage in competition. This, it is believed, keeps prices down, stimulates innovation and encourages the production of a range of goods and services for the public. Monopoly (a word derived from the Greek, meaning single seller) occurs in industries where one company dominates the market. This situation often leads to higher prices, and because there is less incentive for innovation, a potential waste of resources. In the worst cases of monopoly a firm spends a great deal of time and money blocking others from entering the market.

But pure monopolies are rare. What is common, however, is the situation of oligopoly, whereby a group of the largest companies control the industry. In practice oligopoly can be similar to an outright monopoly, for oligopolies often tacitly agree on standards, division of the market and even prices. Most governments have regulations meant to control the worst forms of company collusion and price fixing and thus encourage competition. But at the same time these regulators also attempt to keep industries as stable as possible, especially when it comes to key economic sectors such as steel, oil and gas production, the airlines and railways. For this purpose, a stable oligopoly provides the best balance between competition and chaos. Most media industries under liberal capitalism operate this way. A small number of companies control the ways in which the industry works. Why has this come about? The answer, I think stems from two sets of factors, some economic and some political.

First, within most media industries several economic tendencies encourage consolidation. Some of these are based on the technology. For example, the high initial costs of creating one film, radio or TV program prevents newcomers from entering the market. After the initial production, however, the cost in making thousands of copies falls dramatically. For radio and TV broadcasting in particular, adding new customers costs almost nothing. Thus most media benefit from economies of scale.[2] As in other industries, the benefits of large-scale operations include larger production runs, automated assembly, bulk discounts on materials and a specialized division of labor. This is nothing new: Hollywood itself was founded on these principles just prior to the First World War and although film companies still refer to themselves as studios most observers from the 1920s on saw Hollywood more as a factory – albeit a 'Dream Factory'.

Economic importance

For many countries of the world, cultural industries account for a significant degree of economic activity. Film and television industries employ millions of people. Hundreds of smaller firms survive as supporting links in the supply chain – from construction to food catering, location rentals to printing, from computer software developers to local transportation and extra labor. The distribution and promotion of media products also generates considerable economic activity. This is as true for India's Bollywood and the expanding animation studios in Korea and the Philippines as

The bigs:

World's largest media companies

Time Warner Inc.
The Walt Disney Corporation
The News Corporation Ltd.
Sony Corporation
General Electric Co.
Viacom, Inc.
Bertelsmann AG

World's largest record companies

General Electric
Sony Music Group – includes Columbia, Epic, etc
Warner Music Group – includes Atlantic, Elektra, etc
EMI Group PLC – includes Capital, Virgin, etc
BMG (Bertelsmann) – includes RCA, Arista, etc

World's largest publishers

Bertelsmann AG – selling 40 per cent of trade books worldwide –
including Random House
Pearson PLC – dominant in academic, medical and business books
– includes Penguin, Prentice-Hall, Macmillan, Viking, etc
Time Warner – includes Warner Books, Book of the Month Clubs,
Little, Brown, etc
Walt Disney Corporation
The News Corporation Ltd. – includes HarperCollins
Viacom, Inc. – includes Simon and Schuster

World's dominant film companies and their parents

Warner Brothers (Time Warner)
Walt Disney Pictures – including Miramax
Paramount Pictures (Viacom, Inc.)
Columbia Pictures / Sony Pictures (Sony Corporation)
Universal Pictures (Vivendi)
Twentieth Century Fox (News Corporation)

Sources:
Benjamin Compaine and Douglas Gomery, *Who Owns the Media?* (Lawrence
Erlbaum 2000).
Gillian Doyle, *Understanding Media Economics* (Sage 2000).
Hoovers Guide to Media Companies (Hoovers Business Press 1996).
Robert McChesney, *Rich Media, Poor Democracy* (The New Press 1999).
Toby Miller et al, *Global Hollywood* (BFI Publishing 2001).
Andre Schiffrin, *The Business of Books* (Verso 2000).
The Wall Street Journal, 24 February 2003

it is for Hollywood's contribution to the Los Angeles'
economy. And for countries like Mexico and Brazil
that export their programs, the industry helps considerably in its balance of payments situation.

Source: International flows of selected cultural goods 1980-98 (UNESCO 2000)

Growth in the international trade value of cultural goods

Developing Countries
Developed Countries
All Available Countries

US$ billions

Media industries attract workers at all skill levels. They also provide factory jobs for groups shunted out of declining industrial sectors or those newly urbanized. In Korea, India, China, the Philippines and Mexico the world's animation and computer companies have set up shop, hiring both the skilled and the semi-skilled willing, if not happy, to work for rates far below industry average in Hollywood, California's Silicon Valley or Tokyo.

The media attract investors from all sectors of the economy but are most closely linked to the largest banks, insurance companies and company or union pension funds. Sometimes the profit allure of the cultural industries outweighs the dynamics of political content. In my part of the world the Ontario Teachers' Pension Fund happily controls a majority ownership position in the right-wing *Toronto Sun*, an anti-union paper if ever there was one.

Media expansion

Media firms can expand in three ways: vertically, horizontally and diagonally. Theoretically, at least, these expansions cut costs for the firms involved and allow greater control over all aspects of the process. They also answer to the two prime goals of corporations, the profit imperative and the growth imperative. Shareholders expect profits to rise and so too the value of their shares. Thus a record factory may be closed rather than modernized and an artist dropped rather than developed. Growth means more profit every year, which often translates as, 'pumping out quick-buck anthologies and slashing costs'.[3]

In vertical expansion, a film production company, for example, moves into the realms of distribution and exhibition. In this way it gains control over all key links in the chain. The US film business operated like this during its so-called classical period between the World Wars. Paramount, MGM, RKO, Warner Brothers and Twentieth Century Fox all controlled distribution and exhibition circuits, thereby guaranteeing an audience for their films. In 1948, when they became too powerful, the federal government forced them to divest their US theater chains, but under the current era of anything-goes private enterprise, the film conglomerates have moved back into exhibition once more.

'The media battlefield today resembles Europe in the 19th century, when there were potent nation states but no single super power,' writes *The New Yorker*'s media analyst Ken Auletta. Seven media conglomerates circle around each other like sharks in a tank, each vying for advantage: the movie studios, TV networks, cable companies, phone companies, computer

Growing the company: vertically, horizontally, and diagonally

Vertical growth involves expanding either forward into succeeding stages or backward into preceding stages in the supply chain.
Horizontal growth occurs when two firms at the same stage in the supply chain or who are engaged in the same activity combine forces.
Diagonal expansion occurs when firms diversify into new business areas, thereby forming cross-media entities. ■

companies, technology makers and publishers. Some specialize in content, others try to control distribution, some focus on software and some on hardware.[4]

Today, media companies constantly experiment with various types of vertical integration by taking over 'upstream' (earlier) or 'downstream' (later) phases of the process. Thus TV and radio firms buy into local or regional stations to form networks; cable TV firms buy production companies in order to guarantee a flow of 'product'; publishing companies such as Bertelsmann of Germany, buy into the online division of the US book-store chain, Barnes and Noble.

Another form of expansion involves horizontal integration. This means growth within the same media sector, for example, record companies buying other record companies. Think of this as an attempt to achieve economies of scope in order to secure cost savings, to reach different segments of the market, to engage in multi-product production and to share overhead, administrative or development costs. This kind of expansion has long been a characteristic of the newspaper business, leading to chains and syndicates. The costs of gathering national news, for instance, can be shared among many papers in different cities. Newspaper chains can also negotiate better terms from paper suppliers and can extract higher rates from their advertising customers.

A third type of media expansion – certainly the one that has grabbed the most attention lately – involves diagonal or cross-media integration. The next chapter will look at the technological reasons for this but for now let's consider some of the political and economic reasons. The most spectacular forms of cross-media expansion have involved media firms crossing over into very different media sectors: the gigantic AOL Time Warner deal of 2000, which married internet business with cinema, TV and publishing for example. Canada has experienced a rash of these mergers since the mid-1990s. BCE, parent of the former telephone monopoly, Bell Canada, now owns or controls CTV the country's largest private TV network as well as a group of influential newspapers. Transcontinental, one of Canada's largest printing firms recently acquired a chain of newspapers in Canada and Mexico. In all these mergers or acquisitions – some successful, some disastrous – the owners or managers convinced themselves that a large media empire should sport diverse tentacles and that profound 'synergies' would prevail in each sector. It is easy to see how newspapers and magazines might benefit from sharing the costs of gathering content. Joint ownership of television and newspapers, however, doesn't necessarily lead to increased efficiency. Other cross-media mergers have taken place out of fear or as defensive measures against their competitors. These might be considered part of a long-range economic strategy but they do not necessarily improve economic performance or benefit the public of readers, viewers, or listeners.

Some economists claimed in 2001, following the collapse of the internet business bubble, that this type of convergence in media firms spelled death. Their prognosis was premature. Certainly the buying sprees of some media tycoons and managers, such as Vivendi Universal's Jean-Marie Messier in France and Seagram Corporation's Edgar Bronfman have ended in near economic collapse. Messier was kicked out of Vivendi and Edgar's uncles and father lost billions. Yet, for every failure of convergence the mega-mergers keep on coming. Particularly at the top of the media pinnacle, the empires of Disney, News Corp and TimeWarner now dominate in several media spheres. In publishing, the British-based Pearson and Canadian Thomson transnationals have each made the successful leap from the old media of books and newspapers to information and communication management. Overnight Pearson has become the second largest publisher in the world and Thomson has totally abandoned newspapers to reemerge into direct competition with companies such as Reuters in the information sector.

Political decisions

It is not just economic factors that create media oligopolies. The situation we now face is a direct result of conscious political choices made by government and business elites stretching back to the early years of the 20th century. As Robert McChesney reminds us, our economic systems are far from natural, despite the mythology of the free market, whose high priests deem it to be the 'most rational, fair and democratic regulatory mechanism ever known to humanity, so by rights it should be automatically applied to any and all areas of social life where profit can be found'.[5] Ironically, notes McChesney, speaking of the US situation, 'few corporate sectors have been recipients of government largess as much as the communication industries'. In the 1930s the US government allowed the emerging medium of radio to become a purely commercial endeavor, explicitly rejecting the opposite notion that saw the airwaves as public space. The same handover has recently taken place with the internet. After investing billions of public dollars into the development of the internet through the military and universities the government has now handed everything over to the largest media companies. They have simply inherited it. This took place during the reign of the Clinton/Gore Democrats. There seems to be full consensus among US elites about the natural law of private media.

Other capitalist media systems around the world show the same patterns, whereby the ruling state has encouraged, legislated or passively allowed a small number of media groups, some state-controlled, some private, some national, some foreign, to control the various industries. Although significant variations apply in different countries or regions, none of this could be described as the natural outcome of free

Jack Valenti: the world's most powerful media publicist

In 1963, in Dallas, Texas, a young public relations hot-shot was riding in the Presidential motorcade. After the assassination of John F Kennedy he flew back to Washington with Lyndon Johnson, the Vice President who was sworn in as President en route. In the air, probably somewhere over Kansas, Valenti was sworn in as the new President's first Special Assistant. So begins the extraordinary semi-public career of the world's most powerful media publicist, Jack Valenti. In 1966 Valenti left Johnson to become President of the Motion Picture Association of America. He's still there.

Jack Valenti likes to think big. 'The future of movie entertainment', he states, 'springs from the human condition's grand simplicity. It is this: people, no matter their culture, creed or country, want to be entertained.' He continues, 'In the howling, brawling global marketplace, one fact is illuminated: The American movie, as an attraction to mass audiences, dominates the world.'

Valenti's job requires him to play many roles:

- to develop and propagate the general ideology of the 'entertainment industry'
- to promote the film industry within the US Government
- to defend the industry against legislation it considers intrusive, such as a government imposed ratings system or censorship
- to promote the US industry throughout the world: as he puts it, 'Trade is much more than goods and services. It's an exchange of ideas. Ideas go where armies cannot venture. The result of idea exchange as well as trade is always the collapse of barriers between nations' (MPAA press release, 2000).
- to defend against industry critics, whether from government, lobby groups, or the religious right: 'The customer knows precisely what is attractive and valuable... It is the local citizenry casting their own votes, not the American film industry' (1993)
- to work hand-in-hand with the US State Department and negotiators at the World Trade Organization to break down barriers to US cultural products
- to negotiate with, and fight, other economic interests, such as the computer industry which he sees as complicit in the war on piracy: 'We're breeding a new group of young students who wouldn't dream of going into a Blockbuster and putting a DVD under their coat. But they have no compunction about bringing down a movie on the internet. That isn't wrong to them. Why? I don't know.' He swears: 'The defeat of earthbound and cyberspace thieves is my highest priority in the 21st century.' ∎

Sources: MPAA press releases
Toby Miller et al, *Global Hollywood*, BFI Publishing, 2001.

markets or the only possible consequence of technological change.

Power brokers

When it comes to media, which now possess unprece-
dented power to shape ideas and opinions, media
owners and managers often show a passion for growth
far beyond what might make sense in purely economic terms. As Gillian Doyle states, 'those who control
popular media have the power to make or break political reputations and careers'.[6] Italy's *Mediaset*
television network run by Silvio Berlusconi, the country's right-wing Prime Minister, provides the most
notorious case in Western Europe. After the 1994 and
2001 elections many surveys showed that *Mediaset* stations directly influenced voters. 'Silvio Berlusconi
already controls three of the four main private TV
channels in Italy. When the Prime Minister of a country and its most powerful media magnate are the same
person, how healthy can its democracy be?' asks TV
writer Raffaele Mastrolonardo.[7] Italian media watchers have also speculated that Berlusconi's initial entry
into politics was to prevent the introduction of strong
anti-trust laws. Whatever the case, the intertwining of
politics and the media show that the media are corporations like no other.

However, we should take care not to impose a single
Western model on these relationships. In China, for
example, media businesses – both national and foreign – accept that the Chinese Communist Party keeps
a tight lid on all aspects of media, from production to
distribution to partnership arrangements. In
Venezuela, a country with vocally right-wing newspaper and TV industries, media owners have been
engaged in a vicious struggle with the Government of
Hugo Chávez since the populist leader came to power
in 1998. And in Central America, Angel González
González, known as 'The Mexican', has amassed great
wealth by steering clear of politics altogether, and

keeping his TV and radio stations free of any political or social content as well.[8] Thus, although media owners around the world possess significant powers to influence public opinion and cultural expression their ability to 'set agendas' in specific terms varies.

More choice than ever?

Some scholars have argued that concerns about media concentration and media power are exaggerated. In the case of Italy, for example, it was Berlusconi's TV stations that broke the monopoly of the state broadcaster, RAI. At the time at least, this was a truly popular intervention, bringing with it a much broader range of program choice – much of it trash – but that is an issue for another chapter. The US trade magazine *Broadcasting and Cable News* constantly argues that US 'consumers' now enjoy more media choice than ever before. Instead of the old triad of NBC, CBS and ABC, the upstarts Fox and Warner Brothers have forged new networks to everyone's benefit. (Though with the exception of *The Simpsons* it's hard to see how anyone could be better off through the rise of the Fox network, especially its talk-TV current affairs shows.) Newspaper chains also claim that the proliferation of new information sources through the internet give readers plenty of choice.

Benjamin Compaine and Douglas Gomery in their influential book *Who Owns the Media?* claim that we should, 'Forget any notion that book publishing is languishing... Superstores helped this a great deal, and so

---

Who shot Mr Burns?

'Dozens of people are gunned down each day in Springfield, but until now, none of them was important. I'm Kent Brockman. At 3 pm Friday, local autocrat C Montgomery Burns was shot following a tense confrontation at Town Hall. Burns was rushed to a nearby hospital where he was pronounced dead. He was then transferred to a better hospital where doctors upgraded his condition to "alive."' ∎

The Simpsons, Episode 2F20. 17/5/95

---

has the internet.' They also believe that the European and US TV industries are far more competitive today than ever and applaud the US Government's decision to allow TV networks to own their programming. Elsewhere Compaine states: 'media conglomerates are not as powerful as they seem, for even corporations must respect the discipline of the market. A diverse media reflects the plurality of politics in modern society. This is democracy in action.'[9]

Do these arguments have any merit? Yes, but only in their potential. In truth, satellite, cable and the internet have presented considerable potential to shake up the status quo. This might be more true outside North America and Western Europe. Under authoritarian regimes such as Korea, Brazil, Iran and Libya the underground or tacit introduction of satellite dishes capturing even the commercial fare of Murdoch's empire has functioned as a Trojan Horse of cultural, even political change. Although the infrastructure of mega-computers, data switchers and satellite relays comprising the internet is as tightly controlled by largely US, political, military and corporate elites as any media form ever invented, the flow of content remains as anarchic and potentially disruptive as in its early days.

Hegemony

In Europe and North America the power of the ruling elites seldom appears in its rawest forms. The media play a key role in communicating and creating legitimacy for those in power. Antonio Gramsci, an Italian Marxist writing while imprisoned in the 1920s and 30s, developed a useful concept for describing this situation.[10] He called it hegemony. Hegemony is achieved when the power of the dominant groups in a society appears natural. It is a form of power or rule not limited to direct political control but one where those who have power maintain their position through the creation of a particular world view, one that seems to be based on common sense. Newspapers, TV and radio can be used to communicate the viewpoint of the ruling elites.

This becomes most obvious in times of crisis, such as the Iraq war in 2003, where a closing of the ranks and a shutting down of critical, oppositional, even skeptical views becomes painfully clear. Even the widely praised BBC, which to North American viewers, appeared more distant than other media from Tony Blair's war emerged with a generally compliant position, what one journalist referred to as BBC – 'Basically Biased Coverage'. But hegemony doesn't confine itself to intellectual matters or ideas. It works within everyday culture and seems to provide a frame for understanding experience.

Even in quieter times the media play a leading role in maintaining the status quo, defining the boundaries of political debate and the economic orthodoxy of neoliberalism. Most empirical studies reveal a significant overlap of media owners and managers with the political elite. Thus they are not really doing someone else's bidding – they're just looking out for family.[11]

Contradictions

The media oligopolies are dominant, but they are not omnipotent. Many contradictions exist, especially if we look internationally. For example:

• National media owners may not be in sync entirely with other economic, political, or cultural elites within the ruling class. (The interests of *Televisa* Mexico may now diverge from the old guard of the PRI.)

• Transnational corporations may not be in sync with the countries in which they operate. (The goal of all corporations is to return profits and dividends to their private or public shareholders – national political elites may prefer that those profits remain within the country.)

• Cultural globalization in the form of MTV, Jet Li and *Buffy the Vampire Slayer* beamed into Iran, India, or

China can play a role in undercutting the power of the ruling religious and patriarchal elite.

• Economic neoliberalism, defined as the ideology of free trade, weak government and globalization, is often itself at odds with authoritarian states that may cling to power through their isolation from the larger world.

• The forces of production, such as new technologies, can alter relations among ruling groups, or even the ruling and the ruled, and provide a catalyst for change.

Democracy and the role of the state

Just as the state often functions as a repressive force or simply a mediator of conflicts among economic and political elites, it has sometimes provided a vehicle or site for democracy in the media. In order to survive democratic media requires attention to four sets of issues, all of which require the active participation of the state and vigorous citizen pressure from the bottom up.

Democratic media require an understanding that they should operate according to the goals of public service, which emphasizes universal and affordable access and diverse content. The public service media knows the difference between citizens and consumers. Numerous media sectors operate as fully competitive, innovative, open to newcomers and economically efficient. Unfortunately, that provides no guarantee of diverse content serving the needs of citizens in general, working people, or marginalized groups such as deaf TV viewers, the education needs of children, or the needs of the impoverished elderly. Analysts such as Compaine and Gomery seem to ignore the fact that consumer choice does not always equal pluralism of opinions or diversity of cultural expression.

Democratic media apply the notion of public ownership (or at least control) of resources, for example public rights over the air waves – the radio and TV spectrum – and over communication infrastructures – the long-distance wires and cables. In addition the public should receive a return on investment of public money. For example, many countries have invested colossal amounts of public monies in creating infrastructure, including most recently communication satellites. Yet all too often once the infrastructure nears completion the state simply hands it over to private interests operating largely under a commercial model.

In the case of capitalist or mixed economies democratic media are only possible in situations where new owners and managers can enter the field through the regulation of combines and trusts and where new technologies can be developed to benefit all.

Finally, democratic media concern themselves with the civil and human rights of all media participants. This includes media producers, who must be free from undue government and commercial interference, and free to innovate and raise politically radical, even unpopular issues. It must also include the rights of those usually at the bottom of the pile, the audiences, as members of groups, with an interest in the protection and growth of culture and language, and as individual audience members who should expect to be afforded privacy protection from media intrusion.

The media as cultural industries

Yet in many countries, but especially in the West, the intertwining of political and media elites parallels a growing convergence of state and media interests in general. The media no longer simply communicate or shape ideas and meanings, they now operate as powerful segments of the economy (akin to the steel, agriculture and transportation sectors). For this reason they are called cultural industries.

The media consume huge amounts of capital equipment and labor. For every development in the miniaturization of cheap and 'user-friendly' gizmos (cassettes, CDs, magazines, TV receivers, Walkmans,

PCs and Palm pilots) new levels of astronomical costs get consumed in the harnessing of the most sophisticated science, technology and infrastructure, such as satellites, hi-tech printing, multi-track music recording and distribution apparatus.

The term cultural industry already contains within it a sense that these industries occupy a realm somewhat different from all others. Prior to the mid-20th century such a concept would have seemed an absurd contradiction in terms, especially by those holding to the notion of culture as an elevated form of human endeavor and accomplishment. Thus, it was partly for its shock value that the group of German intellectuals who came together in the 1920s, known as the Frankfurt School, coined the phrase.[12] They saw it as a term of irony and scorn, describing the way in which the mass media were undermining culture. Their concept was to some degree reactionary and undemocratic in the way that it discounted popular taste and new forms of popular culture, largely delivered through and made possible by the mass media. But it also encapsulated a much needed critique of the growing role of capitalist commerce into all areas of social life. Mass culture was at its heart commercial culture. This concern over the spread of commercialism (what McChesney calls hyper-commercialism) has only grown since the 1930s – and not only among crusty European intellectuals.

Business like no other

In some respects the cultural industries behave like other industries and business. They obsess over costs, markets, growth, competition and profit. But in other ways the media do not behave like other businesses. Some examples:

- Television, radio, the internet and newspapers sell content to individual viewers, listeners and readers but they also sell audiences to advertisers. For these reasons media content needs to be managed.

- Most forms of media, but especially TV, radio and the internet enjoy significant economies of scale so that it becomes very cheap or of no cost at all to reach more customers.
- The distinction between originals and copies (or multiples) doesn't apply; no matter how many people read, listen, watch, or surf, the value to each is not diminished. In other words the product is not used up.
- TV and radio have no built-in means of collecting revenue. Until recently, with the advent of cable and satellite Pay TV, broadcasting was a free service.
- Movie theaters rent chairs to their customers, providing an experience – something akin to a medium of transportation, like an airline or railway.
- Some newspapers operate at a loss because their owners want the political influence. This applies to papers right across the political spectrum. In the UK, The Guardian Newspaper Ltd., which operates both *The Guardian* and *The Observer*, is wholly owned by the Scott Trust, whose purpose is to protect the editorial independence of its papers rather than to make profits from them. In Canada, right-wing Conrad Black operated his *National Post* at a tremendous loss; he sold it to the liberal Asper family, who likewise continue its life at a loss but as a mouthpiece for their pointed editorial views.

Symbolic culture and prestige

Cultural industries have symbolic importance to the societies or states where they reside. This allows them to draw support and subsidies, beyond what other industries might expect. Government assistance to its film or TV industries isn't just support for local business and jobs but sustenance for the imagined 'essence' of the state or society itself. A strong link has long existed between healthy cultural industries and national pride to the extent that a beef or lumber industry never could. The cultural industries act as guardians of a nation's culture and to some degree the government's legitimacy.

France French cinema once dominated the world. True, the empire had sunk by the end of the First World War, but the vitality and quality of French film prevailed. Now, protection of its cinema has come to symbolize protection for all other aspects of French life – both as a participant in the European Union and against the US.

India India produces more films than any other country – 800 per year, twice as many as Hollywood. This includes a popular cinema of musicals and melodrama and a smaller but significant cinema of art and social concern. The country supports 12,000 theaters, covering every state and employs directly or indirectly some six million workers.[13]

In contrast to France, until recently India has done poorly in exporting its cinema. Yet, as mentioned earlier, the central Government has used the cultural industry of cinema for three key purposes: to promote a uniform culture; to champion Hindi as the dominant language; and to espouse a secular state.

Britain Unlike France and India, Britain struggled in vain to establish a cinema distinct from Hollywood. The radical cinema of Ken Loach and Tony Garnett, Derek Jarman and Tilda Swinton and the working-class comedies of *The Carry-On* gang and *The Full Monty* just don't cut it for a government intent on building a national symbolic identity.

It's the small screen where all the action has taken place. Here the British (really English) Great Tradition has triumphed by playing on the 19th and early 20th century novel, reaching its peak with the Austen extravaganza in the late 1990s (two *Emma*s, *Pride and Prejudice* and *Persuasion*), the BBC and various private broadcasters have created an idyllic vision of England. However true, and regardless of the individual films – some truly great, some appalling – the TV cultural industries of Britain have greased the wheels for tourism in a way that no ad campaign could ever achieve.

1 John Sinclair et al., *New Patterns in Global Television* (Oxford 1996). 2 Gillian Doyle, *Understanding Media Economics* (Sage 2002). 3 Peter Spellman, 'The real reason record companies suck', http://tetrica.com/misc/bigmusic.html. 2001. 4 Ken Auletta, *The Highwaymen* (Random House 1997). 5 Robert McChesney, *Rich Media, Poor Democracy: Communications Politics in Dubious Times*, (The New Press 2001). 6 Gillian Doyle, op cit. 7 Raffaele Mastrolonardo, 'Media concentration: the Italian case study', in www.opendemocracy.net, 14 March 2002. 8 Rick Rockwell and Noreene Janus,'The Triumph of the Media Elite in Postwar Central America', in Elizabeth Fox and Silvio Waisbord, *Latin Politics, Global Media* (University of Texas Press 2002). 9 Benjamin Compaine, 'The myths of encroaching global media ownership,' in www.opendemocracy.net, 8 November 2001. 10 Antonio Gramsci, *Selections from Prison Notebooks* (Lawrence and Wishart 1971). 11 For the British case, see James Curran and Jean Seaton, *Power Without Responsibility: The Press and Broadcasting in Britain*, 5th edition (Routledge 1997). For the US, see Ben Bagdikian, *Media Monopoly,* 6th edition (Beacon 2000). 12 Theodore Adorno and Max Horkheimer, *Dialectic of Enlightenment*, (Herder and Herder 1972), and a later statement in Theodore Adorno, *The Culture Industry* (Routledge 1991). 13 Manjunath Pendakur, *Indian Popular Cinema* (Hampton Press 2002).

4 Technology: the rise of the machines

'It's useless to invent something that can't be sold.'

Thomas Edison

What is behind my TV and those little wires that disappear into the wall? But think beyond the hardware: the communications technology revolution may be more of a media soundbite than a radical shift in society. Media technologies unfold over long periods and through many stages, performing many functions in business and society. Converging digital technologies affect cultural industries and specific media forms.

ARNOLD SCHWARZENEGGER ADJUSTS his gaze ever so slightly and prepares to darken his voice just a tad. Cyborg man is about to speak. Is he a harbinger of the latest media technology, one that avoids external devices entirely and simply tunes in to the side of one's head? Is this the machine-dominated future we see assembling itself in our era – a time in which technology marches forward seemingly on its own, regardless of our qualms about its effects on human life and society? Or is he simply the ghostly messenger from the old media past, here to announce his plans as Governor of California?

This chapter suggests some ways to think about media technology and looks at how such technology both reflects and changes the media. Many thinkers in this area avoid using the word 'technology' entirely. We should think beyond the hardware, to the ideas, desires, cultural forces – in fact the mythology – that has developed alongside the machines.[1]

Unlike the older arts, the modern media cannot exist without elaborate electrical machinery at all phases of production and exhibition. These media technologies exist almost solely as industrial produc based on advanced science, engineering and precision, large-scale manufacturing. Each stage in the media flow – production and recording, distribution and reception – requires a different set of technologies. In these ways technology shapes the art and shapes the audience, for example, its size and its experience. But how do these technologies come into being?

What will they think of next?
Stages in the development and introduction of new technology

New technologies tend to be both welcomed and feared. Some make communication easier or enrich our experience; others just complicate our lives or throw us out of work. But, whether positive or negative, they are never one day made in the laboratory and the next loosed upon the world. As media historian Brian Winston – who has examined the sequence by which technologies come into our lives – shows, in every case the new device has unfolded over a period of years, even decades. This calls into question the modern idea of a sudden technological revolution.[2]

Winston breaks the process down into five stages: scientific competence, technological application, prototypes, invention and production. The idea of TV, for instance, rests on the scientific knowledge of photoemission, that certain metals produce electrons when stimulated by light. The application of that knowledge led to a long series of prototypes and dead-ends, beginning in the 1920s. Thus the invention stage came relatively late and even then did not guarantee that large-scale production would be possible.

Each stage, says Winston, can be subject to decade-long delays or quick leaps forward, what he calls 'brakes' and 'accelerators'. Machines or devices only become diffused once a strong social, economic or political need for them exists. Thus, he argues, each

... room, sits my $400, somewhat modest, 20 inch Sony, ... in its black plastic, with a slightly rounded screen — from the ... us generation. It looks domestic and simple, with only a couple ...ook-up wires curling down to the floor, disappearing behind Aunt ...arg's bookcase. I've been living with that box and its older cousins for 50 years now. I take it for granted.

But what does it really take to get the thing working? If Alice in Wonderland plunged through the screen to follow the rabbit down the cable and out from the house what would she find on the other end?

Behind that device stands a vast combination of technologies, science, engineering, economic forces, government policies, and international accords. It all seems so effortless: just press the remote clicker, if Angus hasn't chewed it, and there it is, my choice, from Mr. Knightly in *Emma* to *Swap Shop* on local cable.

The Cable Company
– program packagers, leasing space on a satellite, maintaining a shared infrastructure with the telephone company

Technology
– the electron gun, scanning mechanisms, analog to digital converter, cold-type presses, coaxial and optic fibre cables, cathode rays

Engineering Associations
– developers of international standards for achieving compatible equipment
– International Organization for Standardization (ISO), American National Standards Institute (ANSI)

Satellites
– Anik II, developed by Boeing Corporation for Telesat Canada, a government agency
– launched on a French Ariane rocket

An International Labor Force
– involved in the design, manufacture, and assembly of all the hardware, including the set itself (my Sony TV could have been manufactured in one of a dozen countries.)

Science
– electrons, optics, lasers, acoustics

Government Regulators
– in Canada for example, the Canadian Radio and Tele-communications Commission
– managing the competition among multimedia companies, cable distributors, phone companies, satellite companies, etc.
– policing the broadcast frequencies to block unfair competition from the US and local 'pirates'

stage requires the right non-technical conditions to be present before moving forward. The major accelerator is a real or perceived need for the device within society. It works on these prototypes to move them out of the lab and into the world at large. Equal access to a radio broadcasting signal might be a real need – eight-track audio cassettes didn't fit that criteria. Brakes, on the other hand, are a result of the often-disruptive nature of a new technology. For example, in the 1920s the US recording industry saw radio broadcasting as a considerable threat. Fifty years later Hollywood perceived video-tape as a similar scourge. Thus the dominance of the strongest commercial forces contained the radical potential of radio and video.

Citizens, too, can occasionally apply the brakes. Today, many people are beginning to worry about a little gizmo that seems more fashion statement than communication device and possibly a new intrusion into privacy – the wireless video phone. Do we really want the potential to click an instant image of someone, which can be sent instantly via wireless relay onto a webpage and be seen by millions?

Technology rules – technological determinism

Rather than the technology revolutions, on the contrary, most of the new media and communication forms have clearly not transformed the key social and economic relations firmly entrenched since the 19th century.

When we consider the complex and usually drawn-out introduction of new media forms it becomes harder to think of technology as the only factor for change. Modern technology can certainly prove either disruptive or liberating but it does not unfold

---

'It's a dirty little secret in high tech that superior marketing and inferior technology will beat out superior technology and inferior marketing every time.'
Paulina Borsook, *Cyberselfish: A Critical Romp through the Terribly Libertarian Culture of High Tech* (Public Affairs 2000).

in a vacuum and it seldom functions as the lone motor driving the media forward. To see technology as all-powerful and living a life of its own leads us into the conceptual trap known as technological determinism. Its mythology is summed up by Raymond Williams thus: 'Technological determinism is an immensely powerful and now largely orthodox view of the nature of social change. New technologies are discovered by an essentially internal process of research and development, which then sets the conditions of social change and progress. Progress, in particular, is the history of these inventions which "created the modern world". The effects of the technologies, whether direct or indirect, foreseen or unforeseen, are as it were the rest of history.'[3]

A better way to understand the effects of media technology is through its various relationships, with,

Technology brakes and accelerators

Brakes

1. Amortization – companies need to pay off their existing equipment before investing in more
2. Training and retooling costs – new technologies require money to implement for production
3. Bureaucracy – company managers and workers may have set and established ways of working
4. Fear of competition – professionals may feel the need to protect their monopoly of knowledge, which a new technology could undercut
5. Cultural and religious traditions may forbid what the new technology could bring

Accelerators

1. Fear of competition – companies may feel the need to adopt new technology or be outflanked by their competitors
2. Potential for profits
3. Need to reach new markets
4. Planned obsolescence – the need to get old customers to re-buy
5. War – often the biggest spur to technological innovation
6. Urbanization – larger cities allow easier distribution of, for example TV cables
7. Changing demographics
8. Novelty / curiosity / art

for example, the economics of the media industries – its technology and costs, efficiency and labor.

Old media, new technology

Throughout the last century the media spiraled through constant change, in part due to the introduction of new technologies. Here are three examples of how these changes affected the art, the business and the experience for the audience.

Film sound. The introduction of sound, ie synchronized dialog and effects is the subject of one of the hardiest myths in cinema history. Most popular history books cite the first sound film as *The Jazz Singer*, introduced by Warner Bros in 1927. Warners, so the story goes, had been struggling and compared to rivals, their films fared poorly at the box office. The larger studios were releasing big budget, big-cast films well suited to the opulent new movie palaces. Warners needed to turn things around. So they gambled everything in the hopes that movie-goers would flock to sound. The all-singing, all-dancing *Jazz Singer* proved an immediate hit, thus forcing the other studios into a scramble to catch up. The classic musical *Singin' in the Rain* (1952) presents the Hollywood silent-to-talkies myth in its purest form.

In reality, Warners had been working for years, hand-in-hand with their large investors including Morgan Bank and Western Electric. At least two competing systems of sound, one using magnetic, another using optical processes had been demonstrated years before. One major impediment was the lack of capital and dispersed ownership in the film exhibition sector to permit the expensive wiring of theaters for sound. Once that was accomplished in the late 1920s the sound film could be introduced.

Video tape. Brian Winston argues, only partly tongue-in-cheek, that Bing Crosby invented video tape. Here again, the science and technology had been worked out some time before. What was missing was an economic need. Bing was a powerhouse in the world of US prime-time radio: his concert programs drew huge audiences. But Bing faced a problem. In order to reach a national audience living over a three-hour time-zone difference his musicians had to play live twice, once for the East, once for the Pacific. This seemed like a waste and certainly increased his labor costs. Thus audio tape was introduced for network radio. This proved so successful that Crosby's company immediately invested in video tape and in the mid 1950s sold the new technology to network TV. It would take another 20 years for home video to find a need.

Newspaper production. Even though some costs, for labor and printing equipment, have risen and revenues from advertising have slipped, by most accounts newspapers remain enormously profitable for their owners. Nonetheless, owners and managers beholden to their shareholders constantly search for lower costs. In this context the new technologies of computerized editing and design have appeared very attractive. During the past 20 years new jobs have been created in the pre-press work of preparing computer files to be read by the presses. However, many more jobs have been lost as the older technologies of composing type and manual layout have been made redundant.

Media economist Gillian Doyle writes: 'Changes in UK labor laws in the early 1980s that restricted the power of trade unions were instrumental in allowing Rupert Murdoch's News International to finally quash resistance to the introduction of new labor-saving production technologies. The replacement of the old hot metal printing presses with modern cold metal technology and on-screen page make-up software meant that extensive labor costs could be eliminated.'[4]

Most recently, competition from internet sources have shaken newspaper managers. In response many have switched to color printing and have developed online versions of their papers.

New media, new technology

From the 1990s on, people started to distinguish the new media from the old. The new media comprised all those forms based on computers. For those of us on the receiving end, the CD-ROM provided a first taste, followed in rapid succession by the networking of computers and web pages and online magazines, radio, films and TV.

But this active, interactive, open source world of new possibilities which encourages us to see ourselves as producers of art or communicators of useful information now coexists, especially on the internet, with more passive activities of listening to, reading and watching what others have produced. Many of those others comprise the largest commercially driven media firms.

The new media often seem to come to us primarily as user-friendly consumer appliances – smaller, cheaper and smarter at every turn. Standing just behind them however is the rather daunting science of broadband communication, data compression, hi-speed relays and switching, transponders and the wireless universe of satellites (propelled into space, lest we forget, by billion dollar rockets). Four newly harnessed technologies facilitate the new media.

Digital. The science and technology behind most of the new devices is the concept of the digital (meaning literally, 'of numbers'). With digital processes all media can be broken down into small bits of information, which in turn can be converted into the same 'language'. This makes for easy translation from one medium to another. The digital process is usually compared to analog forms of continuous waves, which provide higher quality sounds and images but cannot be broken down into small bits.

Compression. Digital media also lend themselves to compression. Compression technology allows huge amounts of data to be sent more easily in compressed form via cable or satellite and then reformulated to its original size at the receiving end. This becomes key when hundreds of TV and radio stations each want space on a satellite. It also means more quantity and therefore higher profits.

For the PC user software that facilitates the compression of data makes the exchange of large computer files, including music and movies, much easier. The IT industry argues that this 'peer-to-peer swapping' is a 'core net activity'. In vehement rebuttal, the film and music industries call it theft. Some say that this new technology therefore spells the end of the record business. Others, with a better grasp of history, look for a new convergence between the two business groups.

Broadband. Bandwidth refers to the amount of information that can be carried in a given time over a wired or wireless communications link. If you think of information (media sounds, voices, pictures and so forth) traveling through a pipe, the old pipes were like a garden hose; broadband pipes resemble the hose of a firefighter. One type of broadband relies on cables comprised of tiny strands of glass filaments. Thus, each cable can carry hundreds of strands rather than the old cables with only a few wires.

Satellite networks. Communication satellites allow radio, television, and telephone transmissions to be sent live anywhere in the world. Before satellites, transmissions were difficult or impossible at long distances. The signals, which travel in straight lines, could not bend around the round Earth to reach a destination far away. Because satellites are in orbit, the signals can be sent instantaneously into space and then redirected to another satellite or directly to their destination. The satellite can play a passive role in communications like bouncing signals from the earth back to another location on the Earth; on the other hand, some satellites carry electronic devices called transponders for receiving, amplifying, and re-broadcasting signals to the Earth.[5]

A first generation of satellites enabled broadcasters to send their programs to other cities or regions or allowed them to be packaged for re-sale to other broadcasters. A new generation of satellites enables Direct to Home broadcasting.

Satellite broadcasting has served as the vehicle for Rupert Murdoch's Star and Sky TV services to straddle the world and for CNN to become a key news source for millions. It has also allowed smaller countries, such as Canada, to assert its nation-building aims and deliver Southern TV to the Arctic and Brazil to export its news and *telenovela* programs and extend its regional dominance within South America.

Technology: at your service

If we think about technology in relation to social, political and economic activity rather than as an isolated phenomenon, several long-term trends appear. Numerous devices pop into our lives in answer to a small annoyance or modest desire – the remote channel changer, for instance. But if we step back and consider the past century, at least in Western society,

---

Satellites

Eutelstat is one of the world's leading providers of satellite infrastructure. It provides capacity on 23 satellites that offer a broad portfolio of services that includes television and radio broadcasting for the consumer public, professional video broadcasting, corporate networks and mobile communications... Today, with its fleet of satellites, which represents one of the world's largest geostationary orbit systems, Eutelstat reaches into Europe, the Middle East, Africa, Asia, Eastern North America, South America and Australia. Eutelstat transmits more than 1,250 television stations and 700 radio stations to an overall audience of 107 million homes connected to cable or equipped for direct-to-home reception.... corporate partners and sponsors include British Telecom, *Deutsche Telekom*, France Telecom, Hughes Network Systems, CNN, TV *Globo*, Brazil, BSkyB, Volkswagen, Renault-F1, International Herald Tribune and others. Based in Paris, the company employs just over 400 people from 24 different countries. ■

Eutelstat company promotion, 2003

---

we might also see that technological change seems to arrive in answer to large-scale needs or desires.

Technology as solutions to problems. Technology and notions of progress have lived side by side since the early 19th century. Together, they comprise two of the key ideas propelling Western culture. Perhaps nothing encapsulates these twin notions of technology and progress better than that quintessential incarnation of modern media, the internet. Technology can now be presented as the solution – for the busy middle-classes in the developed world and for the computer-deprived (which to Microsoft et al means information-deprived) masses elsewhere – access to the internet holds great promise. In the 1950s and 60s Western elites preached that a poor country's creation of a national radio and TV network marked a necessary stage in achieving a healthy economy and entry into the family of 'developed' nations. Today, it is said, Third World states need to participate in the information and communications revolution in order to be part of the global economy.

Technology for realism. Audiences, critics, and media producers all seem to crave what are perceived to be media forms, styles and conventions that replicate the outside world. This trend toward realism has dominated film, television and recorded music histories. And it's the technology that has made it happen; many film histories begin with a story of the machines. The push toward realism has often been evoked as a natural unfolding of a media's potential. Thus, for many film historians cinema was born with great promise and the grand potential that one day it would be capable of duplicating life. With each new invention the cinema moves to fulfill that promise. Thus color replaces black and white, talking actors replace written dialog titles, hi-fi replaces monaural sound. But not all technologies get taken up. Thus Dolby Sound, which seems to surround us, becomes the norm; Smell-o-Vision does not.

Technology for spectacle. The earliest films from the 1890s based their appeal only partly on their realism; even more attractive was the lure of the incredible, created by the marvels of science. For example,

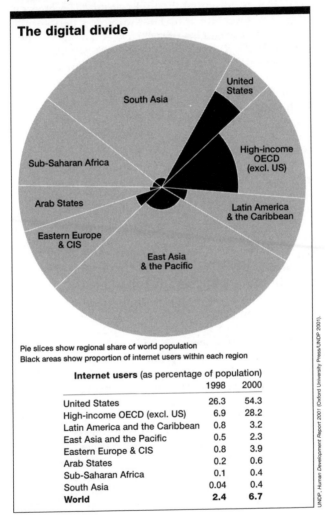

The digital divide

Pie slices show regional share of world population
Black areas show proportion of internet users within each region

Internet users (as percentage of population)		
	1998	2000
United States	26.3	54.3
High-income OECD (excl. US)	6.9	28.2
Latin America and the Caribbean	0.8	3.2
East Asia and the Pacific	0.5	2.3
Eastern Europe & CIS	0.8	3.9
Arab States	0.2	0.6
Sub-Saharan Africa	0.1	0.4
South Asia	0.04	0.4
World	**2.4**	**6.7**

UNDP, *Human Development Report 2001* (Oxford University Press/UNDP 2001).

Edison's promotion people described him as 'The Wizard'. This early aesthetic derived more from the theater, the circus and the magician than the realist novel or photography. Even the most mundane of street scenes presented themselves to the viewer as an attraction. Over the years Hollywood has periodically returned to the cinema of spectacle – in a big way during the 1980s. Today many of the most popular films, especially those that seek a global audience, flaunt their new 'special effects' technologies to create more spectacle than plot.

Technology for privacy. Radio, television, video and personal computers all contain the potential to intrude into our lives. But many of these devices also encourage people to retreat from public life. In a world often seen as increasingly complicated, confusing and troubling, the ability of news and entertainment media to function for us in private can seem ideal. As we live more and more as isolated individuals, known only as consumers by the dominant media, the privacy of media consumption also seems perfect.

The flip side to privacy is the ability to be clandestine. In this way short-wave radio, cassettes, wireless internet and pizza-size receiving dishes allow communications and programs otherwise banned or frowned on by the state or religious authorities.

Technology for crowds. A contradictory impulse to privacy, especially perhaps for young people, is the need to break free to the wider world. Music performance on a mega scale has called into being the electric guitar, the mega-watt amplifier and the JumboTron video screen (not to mention the entire genre of 'stadium rock', from AC/DC to The Three Tenors). Large-scale entertainments also reflect long-term trends to urbanization and the need to stimulate the consumer market. In many countries, both rich and poor, large-scale music performance also allows many more people to participate, a reflection of the high cost of performance in small venues.

Technology for consumption. As individualism and consumption often seem to stride hand in hand, the technology of miniaturization also plays a part. In my youth the transistor radio seemed to liberate us from the parental control of music. Owning devices both miniature and portable provided freedom; they also freed the postwar generations with disposal incomes to spend. This remains true even in some of the poorer regions of the world. Cheap tape decks and cassettes continue to fuel youth cultures, for example for Rai music in Northern Africa.[6]

Technology for surveillance. Miniaturization and two-way communication devices, such as the PC, answer the needs of business and governments to monitor their consumers and citizens. Media businesses sell content. But they also sell their audiences to advertisers. For both purposes the more they know about their customers needs, desires, tastes, family life, work life, activities, educational level, friends, neighborhoods, bank accounts, even voting records, the easier it is to sell them products or sell them as potential consumers to advertisers.

Governments need accurate statistics for all manner of benign purposes such as census data and health records. Unfortunately, governments also like to monitor their citizens for repressive reasons. The ability of the internet and its attendant super-computers to store and sort vast amounts of information provides a new tool for the state.

Technology for war. Media technologies such as the computer itself and the networking of computers that led to the internet, trace their origins, at least in part, to the Second World War and the Cold War that followed. British computers for breaking coded Nazi messages, navy computers for tabulating ballistics (at what angle should a missile be set for its warhead to reach the target), computers in networks for preserving military communications should the enemy stage an all-out attack.[7] The systems for rocket-launching satellites so that we viewers can catch the World Cup live also serve the mad schemes of Pentagon planners.

Technology for globalization. Most media companies need to reach new audiences beyond their immediate territory. The key technologies of satellite communications encourage the creation of an international audience for media products. And the capacity of the newest satellites makes it possible for broadcasters to package different language versions of their programs simultaneously. In addition, devices just beyond the horizon for voice recognition and computerized language translation could also enable the increased flow of international media.

Technology for democracy. Many of the trends outlined above are negative. But despite this, more people in more places now participate in some manner with news and entertainment forms that can vastly improve our lives. As Raymond Williams believed, speaking of newspapers and television in the 1960s, 'the extension of communications has been part of the extension of democracy'.[8]

Even as the ruling elites and large corporations work to contain, control, or manipulate their citizens and consumers, large groups of people steadily create new forms of resistance, new relationships, or simply new methods of using the media for their own purposes.

Converging technologies

In the previous chapters I talked about the expansion of single media companies into multi-media conglomerates. Disney moves beyond theatrical films to converge with ABC into news and television. *Groupo Abril*, South America's largest publishing company dives into cable and satellite TV; printing companies take on publishing; cable TV operators buy production studios; Pearson in the UK becomes a world leader in connecting print and new media with more than 200 companion textbook websites. In all these cases media owners and managers seem convinced that operating in more than one realm will cut costs, develop 'synergies', stave off their competitors, strengthen their national interests and increase profits.

This chapter has shown that the technologies have been converging as well. Is this a coincidence or has one led to the other?

The science and engineering that has brought the methods of digital encoding, compression, broadband and wireless makes it possible to convert one media form into another. Content developed for books and magazines can easily be deposited online or a radio performance can be captured and repackaged for a CD or an internet portal.

The media elites of owners and managers constantly invoke the wonders of technological convergence as the reason for their growth. How much easier it is to say that new technology leads them on to greater heights and broader scope than to invoke the need for greater profits, expanding markets and more control. In the business pages of the *Financial Times* managers proclaim their mastery of the firm, its keen management, its productivity and market share; elsewhere they speak only in awe of the marvelous communications revolution that makes it all possible and inevitable.

Another form of convergence is haunting the world. As a result of both the corporate and the technological trends the lines are beginning to blur in the various media forms themselves. Information, communication, news and entertainment blend into new forms. The personal computer provides a hub of this activity – is it a device for information or entertainment, a source of news or a tool for two-way communication? The older media blur some of their long-established forms as well, so that the TV news and entertainment departments begin to resemble each other. New shows such as *Star Search, Pop Idol, American*

Idol and in Québec, *Star Académie* get developed precisely because of their 'synergistic' potential.

The new technologies of convergence put fear into the hearts of many established media elites. Jack Valenti's good fight against the downloading teenage pirates represents one such concern. And long-established media giants in book, magazine and newspaper publishing certainly dread the growing power of the internet. Old-time TV broadcasters, whether private as in the US, public in Britain and France, or despotic as in Iran and Turkey see their influence slipping in the face of new competitors. In the US the big three networks, NBC, CBS and ABC have seen their market share drop drastically.

Another fear stems from the so-called fragmenting of audiences. Technology that provides more channels to be carried on satellites and into the home allows audiences to break up into niches of interest. New devices, from the VCR in the 1970s to today's concern over music file-sharing via computer invite consumers to program according to their own timetables, endlessly hacking, sampling, or sharing beyond the reach of the corporate elites – beyond the commercials even.

But suggestions that audiences or consumers have 'fragmented' – as if shattering into tiny pieces – is an exaggeration. Although some media firms in the TV and record industries have lost revenues and market share their domination in every media sector remains solid. In 2003 85 per cent of all records sold were released by the big five.[9] Movie attendance is soaring in North America and Europe – in Britain more than twice as many viewers bought cinema tickets in 2002 than ten years earlier.[10]

Are the new media technologies leading to a new economy, a new politics, and new social relations?

Post-Fordist economies. If the old economy was dominated by the ghost of Henry Ford and his assembly line for mass production of industrial goods, some observers believe that a new post-Fordist economy is upon us. In this new era workers need not congregate in large factories and production tends toward flexible specialization. Because the old mass markets are fragmenting, media companies must restructure to produce specialized or customized products for particular markets. This accurately captures the world of the largest multi-media conglomerates. It is less accurate if we look at the world through a national or regional lens. India, the Philippines and Korea have encouraged the creation of large media factories for animation and software production, assembly-lines for the TV and computer giants. Yet for these countries, and the managers and workers of the operations, flexibility seems a distant goal.[11]

Diverse interest groups. If the old politics relied on masses and classes linked in small geographic territories, the new media, it is said, pushes us toward more diversity, the development of communities of interest beyond national borders and a concern over the effects of globalization. True also perhaps for new geo-linguistic audiences across the world. But it is just as true that the new media have widened the existing class divide, where cable, satellite receiving and the internet soar well out of reach.

Better societies. Proponents of the new media come in all political stripes. In addition to the elites, led by Disney's Michael Eisner and News Corp's Rupert Murdoch and egged on by business writers who tout the new economy, many people working for democracy and social change profess high hopes as well. Take the bloggers. To blog is to create and maintain a daily, online diary or weblog, comprised of ideas, stories, manifestos and above all, links to other peoples' weblogs.

'Journalism,' says one blogger, 'is being revolutionized by the latest technology. We have gone from Old Media, through New Media, to We Media: the idea of using the power and the knowledge and the energy of people at the edges.' As journalist Ben Hammersley reports: 'Because bloggers on similar subjects link to each other, the reader finds it easier to understand opposing points of view. On the internet, everyone is the same size – and by allowing experts in their field to correct others and be corrected themselves, almost in real time, blogs release the voice of the readership.' [12]

Hackers, jammers and blogs: the lure of low tech

As the bloggers demonstrate, it's not just high tech that can transform society. Back in the 1960s and 1970s a movement of technological rejection and adaptation gained steam in both rich and poor countries alike. Film and video producers took to Super 8 amateur film and portable video as ways of producing different kinds of personal and political art. At the same time in the Third World engineers, media makers and community workers began to talk about appropriate technology. Appropriate technology was less expensive, easy to repair, built for durability and above all suited to its context. Some of this was simply an accommodation in the face of scarcity, a make-do philosophy where high tech was not available. Radio people, recording artists, and engineers developed new genres with rougher, less polished sounds. Jamaican reggae might stand as the prime example.

But low tech also stimulated better art and more direct and democratic communication. In Cuba following the revolution of 1959 a feisty and socially important documentary film movement, with minimal resources, using found footage, hand-drawn animation and collage became a model for engaged cinema everywhere. The great films of Santiago Alvarez, especially *LBJ*, a savage satire of Lyndon Johnson and *NOW!*, an eloquent film poem on the US civil rights movement, led the way for a political avant-garde in all the Americas, including the US.[13]

Some US computer histories also glorify the hacker culture of the 1970s as a philosophy among nerds and other high-skilled, low-status workers to take control away from those in the US military and other big institutions. Their goal, according to some, was to design operating systems and software that could be freely shared. Their belief was that access to computers should be unlimited and that all information should be free.[14] In their world those people or institutions that would use computers for control or profit, such as IBM and Microsoft, were the enemy.

Technology affects media forms

While technology rarely functions as the sole agent for change, it is shortsighted to ignore its effects altogether. In my example of the way that sound took over Hollywood cinema I emphasized that the sound processes were many years in development and part of a complex set of business strategies not only by the film studios but by the electrical and recording industries as well. Yet, it would be ridiculous to claim that once in motion the sound film played no role in changing all of cinema. The effects proved enormous though not immediate in all parts of the world. Change was required at all stages in the process, from the techniques of acting and staging, to the expensive wiring of theaters for sound. The entire 30-year history of cinema, from 1895-1927, now summed up plainly as the Silent Era, seemed to recede into fog.

So, the world media function as business entities and institutions, with political and commercial structures all thoroughly enmeshed in complex technologies. But what about the media content itself, the media texts? Why, aside from the profits, power and prestige for their owners do they matter so much? What's the attraction for the rest of us? How exactly do various media forms draw us in and under their spell?

In the next chapter I will try to address these questions, beginning with a consideration of media art.

1 Ellen Rose, *User Error: Resisting Computer Culture* (Between the Lines 2003). 2 Brian Winston, *Media, Technology and Society: A History: From the Telegraph to the Internet* (Routledge 1998). 3 Raymond Williams, *Communications* (Penguin 1962). 4 Gillian Doyle, *Understanding Media Economics* (Sage 2002). 5 For a good introduction to communication satellites see the Canadian Space Agency website, www.space.gc.ca 6 See, for example, Philip Bohlman, *World Music: A Very Short Introduction* (Oxford 2002) and Timothy Taylor, *Global Pop: World Music, World Markets* (Routledge 1997). 7 Winston, op cit. 8 Williams, op cit. 9 Compaine, op cit. 10 Doyle, op cit. 11 'Software Industry, Religious Nationalism, and Social Movements in India: Aspects of Globalization,' Ramaswami Harindranath, in Pendakur and Harris, op cit. 12 Unnamed blogger quoted in 'Time to blog on', Ben Hammersley, *The Guardian*, 20 May 2002. 13 For an overview of the Cuban cinema see Michael Chanan, *The Cuban Image* (British Film Institute 1985). 14 Rose, op cit.

5 Art and audience

'We now have the sociology, it is sometimes said, but where is the art?'

Raymond Williams[1]

The media are the vehicle for most artistic expression and communication in the modern age. They have also amplified, extended and transformed artistic forms and practices. All the media arts are constructed forms, with meanings partially shaped by the interpretations and responses of 'active' audiences. Audiences differ across the world and depending on their social composition.

THE OLD NOTIONS of art have been under attack and crumbling for more than a century. Great amounts of ink have been spilled arguing for the state of film, radio and TV as arts. But perhaps the crucial question is whether these media have overturned the entire notion of art. As Walter Benjamin asked in the 1930s: 'What becomes of the aura surrounding a work of art in the age of mechanical reproduction?' Since then recording and reproduction technologies have multiplied to the extent that for most of us contact with an original work of art is rare compared to our contact with works in which the concept of an original has no meaning. The 20th century stretched the boundaries of acceptable art, not simply its subject matter and settings, but in the more radical question of who gets to be called an artist. Many artists themselves, working in both traditional and new media, have deliberately set out to shock their audiences by addressing these basic questions. Each generation since the 1880s has believed that it has overturned the conventions not only of their immediate elders but everything that has come before.

And yet, again following Raymond Williams, the attempt to identify art (and the aesthetic) is itself an extraordinarily important historical and social process. So the debates should continue even if they will never be settled.

Many people in the media remain happy enough to describe themselves as craftspeople, technicians, or cultural workers. The media as institutions however, draw at least some of their legitimacy from their status as art forms. This holds true for certain types of journalism as well. In some academic circles the notion prevails that art itself, as an elitist and exhausted concept, has been demolished once and for all. Elsewhere, our Ministers of Culture (or Heritage), museums, galleries, and auction houses are booming – for some the religion of art has never been healthier.

Some of this spills over into the media products themselves with biographies of great writers, painters, musicians and new versions of the classics. Yet by and large this sort of highbrow fare occupies only a small slice of the media pie. It's the Top 40, John Grisham, and *The Hollywood Squares* that really bring in the cash.

Despite modern media's reliance on technology and complex structures, they also rely fundamentally on inherited forms of artistic expression and communication – some forms of storytelling, language, music, theater and performance stretching back thousands of years.

We watch, read, listen and download because *we like it*, even if coercion or lack of other choices also comes into play. We recognize, as do the elites who own the cultural industries, that media products speak to us and affect us differently from other products. These products deal with symbols, created and circulated to speak not only to our basic needs but to our desires and imaginations.

No study of the media in all their complexity can move forward without an understanding of these symbolic forms, which for better or worse we normally refer to as media art.

Nusrat Fateh Ali Khan (1948-1997)

Nusrat Fateh Ali Khan stands in the eyes of many as the 20th century's most inspiring singer. Almost single-handedly he brought the music known as *qawwali* to the world. *Qawwali* is the devotional music of the Sufi faith, traditionally performed only at the shrines of Sufi Muslim saints in Northern India and Pakistan. Nusrat's followers believe that his family of *qawwali* singers stretches back six centuries to the beginnings of Sufism as a mystical sect of Islam.

From the 1960s on Nusrat performed in hundreds of concerts world-wide. His many recordings highlight the distinct *qawwali* sound based on a chorus of male voices and complex rhythms of hand clapping. The recordings range from strictly traditional and devotional songs, often live in a spiritual setting, to compositions and performances of fusion mixing Brazilian *surdu* and Senegalese *djembe* drums. Above all Nusrat's voice soars with incredible power and energy, an effect that many listeners describe as spiritually inspiring regardless of their beliefs.

In the West his name reached superstar status through his soundtrack work in the films *Dead Man Walking* and *The Last Temptation of Christ*. But he himself always made it clear that the music had different functions depending on the setting; as music within Sufism and as Sufi music.

The music scholar Philip Bohlman described the tension in Nusrat's music between transformation and restoration: from the sacred to the secular, from the classical to the popular, from traditional to fusion, from devotional to public. But what emerged were multiple rather than single directions. Nusrat shows, says Bohlman, that in world music 'tradition returns again and again, not to be used up or relegated to the past, but to be restored with new meanings in the present.' ■

Sources:
Philip V Bohlman, *World Music: A Very Short Introduction* (Oxford 1992).
Jameela Siddiqi, 'Nusrat Fateh Ali Khan' in *Songlines*, September/October 1992.
Traditional Sufi Qawwalis, Live in London, Navras Records, NRCD 0016/17, 1993.
Nusrat Fateh Ali Khan, *Mustt Mustt,* Real World Records, 7862212, 1990.

Five elements of media art

Entertainment. The statement that something is 'only entertainment' holds great sway when people talk about media forms – usually in contrast to education or something 'serious'. But the various forms of media art force us to take entertainment seriously. First off entertainment is not such a simple concept. Certainly, it is not difficult to think of some media forms so mindless that extracting any value seems pointless.

The *World's Best Police Chases* might qualify, or the comic strips in the Sunday newspaper, or a tawdry murder mystery on sale in the bus station. I, for one, have no difficulty in trying to set criteria for judging quality. The difficult issue becomes sorting out another person's idea of taste from our own. To take the cases above, many of the world's greatest novels have involved a chase and murder; some of the world's finest modern art shares the simple iconography and color of the comics; and who would say that comedy contains no value beyond plain entertainment?

In any case, the so-called serious forms seldom banish entertainment entirely. Documentary films treating the most serious of subjects provide entertainment by focusing on characters or the small details of overlooked life. Modern documentaries embrace many of the devices of narrative fiction, including surprise, suspense and conflict. In fact, most serious art, whether experienced through the mass media or in more traditional settings, diverts our attention from work and daily worries. When the middle classes attend the theater or tune in to *Classics by Request* is there no connection between contemplation and entertainment?

The media industries themselves often use the rhetoric of entertainment when it suits them. Many social critics also frame their critique in these terms. But is entertainment, even in the popular sense, a negative pursuit? If we think of entertainment as emotional nourishment of similar value to the literal nourishment of food and drink, does every meal need to qualify as gourmet fare? Do we cast aspirations on eating and sleeping because they distract us from more 'serious' endeavors?

Pleasure. If entertainment seems passive, the idea of taking pleasure connotes a more active engagement. Pleasure takes many forms: pleasure in seeing one's life mirrored in a book or on-screen; pleasure in learning about other people and cultures; pleasure in solving an enigma in a narrative; pleasure in acquiring a sense of aesthetic form or recognizing the skill of a craft.

Some derive pleasure from the technical apparatus itself, as one newspaper critic wrote in 1953: 'There is something intrinsically pleasurable about the whole process of selecting, buying and playing a record. Indeed the hi-fi enthusiast probably derives as much pleasure from extracting the record from its sleeve, carefully cleaning its surfaces, and adjusting the controls of his hi-fi, as from listening to the music.'[2] Younger readers smirking at the ancient technology might pause to consider the zest of the computer buff downloading their MP3s (the dismay of Jack Valenti notwithstanding).

Distraction. What the masses need in hard times is distraction. Wasn't that how people got through the Depression – glued to the radio and flocking to the movies? Here is another complex word masquerading as a simple one, for class bias often plays a part when distraction comes up. Sometimes it seems that when rich folks take time off they take part in recreation and leisure; poor folks should concentrate on 'bettering themselves' – indulging in the genres of popular media can only be considered a distraction. Social critics who look to the working class to lead us to the future have often bemoaned the media in these terms, as a new opiate of the masses.

In traditional views of Western art which remain deeply ingrained, the production and appreciation of art must be seen as 'work'. The rewards for both the artist and the audience should not come easily – that's partly what gives great art its value, for it is rare. In these terms those forms of media that do not seem to take much effort to 'consume' hardly qualify.

Utopia. A justly celebrated essay on film theory by Richard Dyer took up the old idea of utopia as a way of disputing those critics who see only distraction in the dominant cinema. In 'Entertainment and Utopia', Dyer charted the many ways that mainstream musicals create a parallel world where everyday problems get resolved and where community wins out over selfishness.[3] These utopias, he argued, could become the source of active aspirations for the audience, perhaps comparing their present world to something better and worth striving for.

A world of scarcity, exhaustion, dreariness, manipulation and fragmentation might be replaced in the utopia by abundance, energy, excitement, openness and community.

Here was a genre that rejected the standard refrain of, 'There is no alternative'.

Education. In addition to media consumption, the thirst for 'adult education' ranks high in our era as a leisure-time pursuit. The media recognize that need and often speak in the language of education even when promoting their routine fare. Nevertheless, educational programming in the best sense does exist. A great number of excellent nature documentaries sit comfortably in the prime-time schedules of broadcasters around the world. Sizeable and growing quantities of serious fiction and non-fiction literature find a place in publisher's lists with increasing book sales to match. And on the internet surfers can find thousands of specialized web sites featuring the visual arts, poetry, fiction, and music from everywhere. These alternate sources of art would have been difficult, if not impossible for all but the specialist to find just five or ten years ago.

The straightforward conclusion is that none of these viewing, listening, reading, or surfing states of mind or activities exclude the others. Humans seem capable of walking and talking simultaneously; capable also of operating on the constantly shifting sand of mixed motives. Entertainment and education can, it seems, work very well together.

Art and commerce

The enormous wads of money involved in the media makes art creation seem like a contradiction.

Commercial pressures can bear down heavily and lead to:
- cutting corners
- reliance on too few people
- cheaper quality materials
- deadline pressures
- censorship (the fear of offending sponsors or customers)
- market censorship – selection based on costs of production rather than innovation

All this can save money but countless media products lose extraordinary amounts of money, despite the best planning.

Art and industry

How can mass media produce anything other than mass art? Isn't this really art by committee with a specialization and division of labor that saps creative vision?

Structurally, the media industries work on a division of labor involving owners and producers; technical people and creative people. The media often rely heavily on a broad range of suppliers, including freelance and commissioned creators. This makes for

Tin Pan Alley existed as a real place for only a short time, but as a metaphor for production-line music it lives on in fine health. At the beginning of the 20th century New York music publishers grouped together on 23rd Street. Critics quickly observed that the publishers had perfected the practice of manufacturing songs by assembling ready-made parts in new permutations.

complex relationships, with each group's outlook and interests slightly different. The production process thus remains far less regimented than in other industries. In the end, although media industries must rely on standardization they fail without innovation.

The market does reward innovation (or at least the appearance of it). Even under capitalism markets and commercial relations never operate in a pure fashion. They constantly react to pressure from political, social, and cultural forces. This is what I referred to in earlier chapters as the political economy. New forms of communication and expression bubble up or overflow their strictly commercial boundaries. New technologies emerge that introduce contradictions, conflicts, or discrepancies.

So, although the media arts operate in industrial and commercial contexts many of their characteristics originate outside those contexts or go on to acquire symbolic meanings beyond their function as products.

What have the media done to art?

In the course of marrying art to modern industry and capitalism the media have fulfilled three roles.

Amplify. The media take existing forms (the novel, theater, music, fine arts) and broadcast these to a much broader audience. This dissemination of what we might call the great traditions should not be overlooked. It has formed part of the extension of democracy and enriched millions of lives. Not only have the classics come to the masses; the range of older folk arts has been vastly expanded as well.

Extend and replace. The media take existing forms and ways of experiencing them and extend or stretch them. For instance, film, radio, and TV take over from the settings of older arts – the concert hall, theater, art gallery – as the new major dramatic and musical institutions. If audiences today hear the literature of traditional India and China or the music of the Andes they will probably hear them on TV or cassette.

Transform. The media also take existing forms and transform or reshape them. Thus the recording industry has not simply replaced musical notation (which for most music never existed) it has for the first time actually *reproduced* the music (and sound). Most music is aural, fleeting, for one-time – now it becomes an object, permanent, endlessly repeatable. This is totally new. Of course, these transformations may or may not produce better forms, just different ones.

Genre

Genre, from the French word meaning type and the Latin, *genus*, is a concept used to group types of art or media forms that share several traits and conventions with others. These conventions of theme, style, plot, effects, etc., have developed over time, and what is crucially important the traits are recognized, and expected, by both the makers and the audience. Examples include musicals, comedies, daytime melodrama (soap operas), news broadcasts and documentaries; in music, Top 40, rock, rap, opera, jazz and so on. On the internet, perhaps the home page and the blog would now qualify.

Most genres appear as completely natural and operate for us unconsciously. Think however about the unsettling effect if only one minor element gets changed – say the cowboys wear fedoras, the TV anchor reads the news from a lawn chair, the pop singer croons in Latin.

The dating genre on Chinese TV: hit shows 1997 – 2001

Special Man and Woman	*Everlasting Romance*
Romantic Meeting	*Golden Meeting*
Saturday Meeting	*Good Man, Good Woman*
The Square of Kindred Spirits (fans of Anne of Green Gables take note)	*Who Does Your Heart Beat For?*
	Conjugal Bliss
	Talking Marriage
Tonight We Become Acquainted	*Heavenly Bliss*

This shows how genres are socially constructed, according to certain ideologies. New and different sorts of media forms seem strange and ill-fitting and face a difficult task in finding a spot and acceptance, by both producers and audiences.

'It is clear that certain forms of social relationship are deeply embodied in certain forms of art', says Raymond Williams.[5] Think, for example, of the history of European drama, moving through Greek Tragedy, English Renaissance, French Comedy of Manners, 19th

Brazilian *telenovelas*

TV came early to Brazil – in 1950. With a population of 160 million and 110 million TV viewers by 2000, the commercial stakes and the social impact of television are enormous. From 1964 until 1985 the military ruled Brazil. A key goal was to construct a national communication network, including TV, as an instrument of national control via national integration. *Globo* TV, though privately owned, became that network and the cornerstone to their success was the melodramatic form known in South America as the *telenovela*.

Brazilians watch a lot of TV, comparable to North American rates of four to six hours per day and in the prime evening hours the *telenovela* in its various forms totally dominates. Like the US soap opera and similar forms produced in Mexico and Nigeria, the Brazilian shows deal with long, complex story-lines centered on a bedrock of love, relationships and strong emotions.

But there are significant differences between the Brazilian *telenovela* and the US soaps. In Brazil the programs run in the evening rather than the afternoon, pulling in a far broader audience and hence the ability to shape social discussion. As a form they are based on daily chapters, with dozens of mini-crises in the plot to keep the viewers coming back, as in the US. But there is a crucial difference: in Brazil the stories end – usually after five to eight months and 160 chapters. Another important difference is that many of the Brazilian shows deal with class difference, even class conflict.

Over the 30 years of their lifetime the *telenovelas* have circled through three broad stages: a romantic period during the dictatorship, a realist phase coinciding with the first years of parliamentary democracy in the 1980s, and a more recent post-realist phase, which some writers believe reflects the needs of *Globo*'s export market and an international audience. For Brazilians today the three stages have become sub-genres, happily coexisting at different evening time slots.

Jesús Martín-Barbero, one of South America's leading media schol-

century Bourgeois Drama. Genres can be traditional or modern, commercial, religious, social, or professional.

The functions of genre

Genre may be the key term in understanding media content. Genres form the bedrock of the media industries and also provide audience members with the basic means for our entry into media art (and purchasing decisions).

Genres function in modern capitalism (both in the

---

ars, suggests that we take these shows seriously and emphasizes that, 'media and communications do not just influence daily life – they are daily life'. He believes in the active viewer: 'Culture is a process that is productive of meaning, and not just a "circulator" of information. Thus the receiver is not just a decoder... but also a producer.'

Telenovelas, despite their stereotypical and distorted expressions, represent true problems – types of problems usually absent in telejournalism. On the one hand, says researcher Thomas Tufte, *telenovelas* work as commercial exploitation and 'ideological training', however they can also 'liberate social energy and tension' which in turn enriches lives and can prompt 'social indignation'.

The Rubbish Queen

'Who has the power in society? Those who have money or those who cultivate their family name? Who is the most important in society? A businesswoman who made her fortune by working in a small second hand shop,... or a society woman, who figures daily in the gossip section of the newspapers and who accepts numerous invitations to dinner, just to be able to eat at least one decent meal a day? One has money but no social prestige. The other, a big name, but not a penny.'

Globo press release for the launch of *The Rubbish Queen*,
March, 1990.

'[The Rubbish Queen] was really good, superb. It was a novela that taught people a lot. The people that are losing, they must not collapse, they have to hold up their heads. We must never bow our heads, must always go with our heads held high.'

Matilde, a viewer from Calabar *favela*, Salvador, Brazil.

Sources:
Thomas Tufte, *Living with the Rubbish Queen* (University of Luton Press 2000).
Jesús Martín-Barbero, *Communication, Culture and Hegemony* (Sage 1993).
Robert C Allen, *to be continued... Soap Operas Around the World* (Routledge 1995).

West and China as well) as a key means of organizing the vast array of media products being produced. Like auto and dog biscuit manufacturers, companies need to standardize their production processes. They can't allow writers and directors to reinvent the wheel every time they enter the studio. Companies also need to feel certain that a large group of consumers will want what they produce. This standardization and need to reduce risk is answered by the development of commercial labels – now usually referred to as branding. One writer describes genre as a form of regulated difference.[6] In other words, genre allows for small innovations and change but within a system that can control the key economic elements of production and distribution.

Another function of genre might be considered ideological. Newspapers, for instance, include both news reports and editorials. In the case of news reports the genre conventions remain hard and fast. An objective, third person point-of-view predominates; opinions from the reporter remain hidden. The structure of the inverted pyramid puts the major factual information at the top – the who, what, where and when. The reporter puts all dialog into quotes and never inserts what a 'character' might be thinking. This so-called objective style of reporting functions to establish the credibility not only of the reporter but the newspaper itself and its owners in general. It is a genre of professionalism. It comes into existence when newspapers operate primarily along commercial rather than narrowly political lines.

But even in traditional papers, news reports get called stories. This story-telling element has been moving up in status. In the West beginning in the 1970s a new genre of creative non-fiction emerged. One writer describes this approach as using fiction techniques in the crafting of nonfiction. These reporters tend to write scenes and focus on 'characters'. In the biggest departure reporters usually insert themselves into the scene, either as observers or even as participants. Most mainstream documentaries now employ this style as well.

Another type of newspaper writing, known as watch-dog journalism, has rapidly developed in South America following the collapse of the military regimes that ruled in the 1970s and 80s.[7] Watchdog journalism works to uncover political and economic wrongdoing among the powerful. The goal, clearly understood by the writers and their readers, is political.

Forms in motion – dominant, residual and emergent

Forms, genres and the practice of art creation never remain static. They change with time. But the change is not one of orderly progress or organic growth, or decline from classic to decayed. Different modes of operating co-exist – new forms, genres and creative practices do not always totally displace what has gone before. One way of thinking about change is in terms of dominant, residual and emergent forms.

Dominant. In cultural production the conditions of dominance are usually clear, in certain dominant insti-tutions and forms, says Raymond Williams.[8] These may present themselves as unconnected with dominant social forms, but the efficiency of both depends on their deep integration. Think, for example, of the tel-evision newscast, the newspaper editorial, the harsh rigidity of Top 40 radio.

Residual. This describes work made in earlier and often different societies and times that remains available and significant. The drama as performed in a theater setting is one example. Music played during Sufi religious cer-emonies is another – a form that co-exists with Sufi music as a 'world music' entity of its own.

Emergent. New meanings, new practices, new rela-tionships continually appear. This often takes place in conjunction with the rising fortunes or aspirations of a particular social class or group in society. In our era the worldwide emergence of a women's movement has provided the seeds for an equivalent emergence in all manner of media forms. In the short run, of course, it remains difficult to distinguish between what is merely the next novelty in the dominant culture and what could be truly emergent.

What is the appeal of cross-cultural forms?

Hollywood. Over the years many explanations (aside from political and economic ones) have been put forward as to why Hollywood cinema remains popular internationally. One of the oldest theories still advanced today is that Hollywood cinema reflects the polyglot culture of US society. In other words, US culture tells stories designed to appeal to the vast array of its immigrants with different ethnic and racial backgrounds, different histories and languages. A prime example is Charlie Chaplin's portrayal of the 'little man' on the outside of society, which struck a nerve worldwide. These stories therefore translate well when exported.

Another theory emphasizes the appeal of Hollywood's opulence and the spectacles created through big budgets. According to the old adage, what counts is 'money on the screen'. No other national cinema could consistently compete. This relates to the belief that Hollywood appeals because it shows the good life, life as it could or should be – a utopia. This utopia can function as a vehicle for harmless dreaming or for unrest, stimulating viewers to compare their lives with those on the screen.

A third hypothesis argues that Hollywood cinema is 'transparent'. Transparent films are deliberately ambiguous. They have 'the capability to seem familiar regardless of their origin, to seem part of one's culture, even though they have been crafted elsewhere'.[9] As commodities, films must appeal to everyone, or at least offend as few people as possible. In consequence, audiences from other countries and cultures find it easy to see their own lives or cultural myths reflected in the films. For example, some writers have claimed that the US soap opera, *The Young and the Restless,* shares properties with the Trinidadian calypso term *bacchanal,* 'which simultaneously means scandal, confusion, and bringing the truth to light'. In Trinidad, therefore, the show can be viewed as if it were indigenous and realistic. This may account for its tremendous popularity.

African American popular musics. More even than Hollywood, perhaps, Black American music in its many forms – jazz, blues, R&B, rock and rap – has conquered the world. Early commentators during the 1920s dubbed jazz the quintessential 20th century form, reflecting and appropriate for modern urban life. Other theories stress how most forms of Black music appeal to international audiences because they represent authentic roots and a revival of music that predates industry and commerce.

African American popular music also represents for many the ongoing failure of the American dream, a confirmation that the US model will not work for other societies. For others, especially youth, Black music represents rebellion, even revolution.

Grl applies to join Asian rock royalty

The word 'Grl' looks like it could do with a vowel. But it's actually the name of a Chinese rock star and means 'the light of wisdom' in Mongolian. Grl is from the grasslands of Inner Mongolia and aims to ignite the Asian music with her talent for song and dance.

Grl took two years out before declaring her return to the pop world this week with the release of her second album Finding. The launch was a chance for her to air the songs in public for the first time. The latest album is produced by a team of Asian rock stars including big Taiwan pop name Wu Bai. It's designed to transform Grl into Asia's Queen of Rock.

She wrote all the songs on the latest album and produced three songs with the help of her band. It took Grl two years to produce this album. You judge whether it was worth the wait. ■

Promotion on China Central TV, Channel 9, CCTV.com.
11 August 2003 13:08:21.

Bring in the audience

In the previous section I discussed general factors that draw people to media art such as pleasure, education and entertainment. I also discussed the concept of genre as a key production tool for media companies but also as crystallizing an historical relationship between media forms and audiences. I ended with a brief survey of the appeal of cross-cultural forms for international audiences. Now seems the time to look at actual audiences more closely.

Are we all just couch potatoes? Before anyone states an opinion about the modern media they have usually formed some sort of theory about audiences in general. Occasionally that theory is conscious, often it's not. Many social critics, from the left to the right of the political spectrum, talk about media audiences as passive. This can be a judgment about the innate nature of people or about the effects of the media themselves. Regardless, much of what follows in their social or cultural criticism flows from that belief.

Even the radical German playwright, Bertolt Brecht, a staunch believer in the masses and popular art, believed that most theater and cinema audiences simply throw themselves into the current of the narrative and drift along with whatever is presented to them. His epic theater of the 1930s sought to interrupt that drifting with devices that would startle or alienate. These effects, he argued, would help create an active audience.

Most theorists involved in media studies now believe that audiences participate in creating the meaning of any media form. In other words to some degree they take an active part, not only in decoding meanings within the text but in actually constructing those meanings. However, 'active' can mean many things.

Theories of the active audience. Let's start with a reminder that the audiences for media products are huge but also diverse and fragmented. In addition we should think of our own relations with the media and remember that we probably watch, listen to, and read a great variety of forms. In the same evening, for instance, we might be part of a massive, worldwide audience for a news broadcast or sports event, then later as part of a minuscule minority with an interest in a locally produced cable show. Thus the term mass audience needs special care.

Like good dinner guests, people watch whatever is put in front of them. That's a standard comment. This could be construed as evidence of passivity; it could also signify a making-do or an adjustment to limited choice.

Why we watch, listen, read, and surf

Once we accept that audiences do more than simply take in messages sent out from media forms we might ask the question: 'What purposes do the media serve in our lives?' One tradition that has taken this up has been called the Use and Gratifications approach. These theorists argue that people's needs influence how they use and respond to a medium. Some of these uses include the need or wish for information, personal identity, integration and social interaction and entertainment. Some of these uses may compensate for needs that the rest of social life frustrates.[10]

Critics of Use and Gratifications theory focus on its individualistic approach and its tendency to exaggerate active and conscious choices. A more modest approach, sometimes referred to as *reception theory* asks the questions 'What do users see in the media?' and 'What meanings do people produce?' The key point for us is that these theories all emphasize that people interact with media for different reasons.

How we watch, listen, read, and surf

Many theories attempt to explain how we as individuals try to make sense of various media forms. Two basic approaches mix physiological and psychological processes.

Gestalt. The Gestalt psychologists, writing in the early 20th century, believed that human perception tends to group things into simple units: 'If the brain were not continually on the lookout for objects, the cartoonist would have a hard time. But in fact all the artist has to do is present a few lines to the eye and we see a face, complete with an expression. The few lines are all that is required for the eye – the brain does the rest: seeking objects and finding them whenever possible.'[11]

Cognitive. A cognitive approach starts from the premise that we seek to make sense of the world, including media forms, through the testing of hypotheses and drawing inferences.[12] These hypotheses are shaped by what we already know, many not limited to vision per se. Objects have pasts and futures. We tend to accept, for instance, in perceiving motion that larger objects stay steady while smaller ones are moving.

Gestalt and cognitive theories go some way in persuading us that the world is not simply 'out there' but is constructed by us as individual and social beings.

Physiological factors as to how we interact actively might include our responses to light and dark, and to loudness and pitch of sounds. Another active trait is the ability of our eye and brain working together to see the motion in motion pictures when what is passing by is a very rapid series of still images each separated by blackness. Most scientists believe that our heart rate can be affected by the rhythms heard in music. It may be that the rapid editing of images can have the same effect.

Psychological factors could include the process of tension and release, or catharsis, often generated by the devices of narrative story-telling. These include the creation of a puzzle or mystery that later gets resolved and the withholding of information from us as viewers or from characters. The psychology of identification provides another way of talking about the active audience. Identification can be with characters in specific situations or as a kind of mirror effect of attraction to others 'like ourselves'.

These theories provide useful approaches and partial explanations. But we should take care not to generalize or turn these processes of the eye and brain into essential categories fixed for all time. All the factors listed have been shaped through history, through societies and through culture. Even our bodies change over time – both human bodies over the centuries and our own over a lifetime. Reaction time to external stimulus, for example, can be subject to training and also to decay. Finally, we must be careful not to extend what we might accept as universal processes, such as heart rate or sensitivity to strong light, into more complex social categories. Ask yourself: 'Do all cultures react to the following in the same ways: babies, landscapes, compositional patterns, story telling?'

Dominant / negotiated / oppositional. Even with this profusion of theories, discussion of active versus passive remains somewhat dualistic, as if we behave either one way or another. It's as if we occupy one of only two states: either lounging half asleep in front of the boob tube, or sitting straight, eyes clear with pencil and notebook in hand. Clearly a range of responses might be at work.

In an attempt to get beyond the rather limited active-versus-passive debate, the British theorist Stuart Hall has argued that all media texts involve a process of encoding and decoding.[13] In most cases the forms of mainstream media get encoded with the dominant world view held by its creators and owners. However, in the subsequent process of decoding viewers may respond to these texts in one of three ways. First, they may accept the dominant world view of the text and decode in the manner intended. Second, they may in a somewhat active manner negotiate with the text, perhaps by accepting the basic legitimacy of the dominant but disagreeing with some of the details. Or third, they might adopt an oppositional stance where they not only reject the dominant ideas in the text but also the entire worldview behind it.

Hall's theory provides one explanation as to why viewers arrive at different interpretations. The theory seems inadequate however in the face of the transparent text or if we consider those many sorts of film, popular music, or television that include irony, contradiction or just plain confusion. In other words, not all texts are perfectly shaped vehicles for delivery of the dominant world view. Most cannot contain all the loose ends or control all the connotations that could arise. For example, most rock and rap songs contain the most conventional ideas about love, lust and relationship; at the same time the exuberance of their sometimes rough instruments, rhythms and styles seem to overwhelm those lyrics and carry for many the

Nigerian video films

In the early 1990s the small feature film movement in Nigeria collapsed, like many other parts of the economy and society. Into the breach stepped a new generation of producers willing to make do with the low tech world of video. Today, more than 600 feature length 'video films' get released each year. It's a strictly commercial and cut-rate business. Budgets rarely top $5,000, shooting seldom lasts more than two weeks, but the finished work often reaches two to four hours. Some distributors claim to sell more than 500,000 tapes per year.

Many of the country's intellectuals and older filmmakers decry their cheap quality, addiction to crime and glamor and lack of social comment. While Nigeria spirals deeper into poverty, nearly falling off the world economic map, the most common icon in the video films is a Mercedes Benz.

The video films quickly gained immense popularity throughout Nigeria with production especially strong in the Yoruba and Igbo languages. Four genres of story currently hold sway: voodoo or ghost stories, love stories, historical epics and gangster stories. There is some controversy over the voodoo genre and the censors frown on it by outlawing cultism, witchcraft, voodooism and the occult. Newspapers and magazines cover the video films with heated and extensive articles. This has led to healthy debates over quality and appropriate subject matter and in some cases prompted higher budgets and better production values.

Like the *telenovelas* of Brazil, Mexico, Colombia and Egypt melodrama

torch of rebellion to the status quo.

Hall's theory also does not explain why people would choose to, or be able to decode in different ways. To explain that we need to recognize that the interpretations which viewers, readers and listeners bring to the media texts are not unlimited.

Flesh and blood audiences

When we move from individual audience members in the abstract all separately lounging, gratifying, interpreting or decoding, to *groups of people* engaged with the media, we quickly confront the fact that people live within social groups. And these groups are partially defined by race, ethnicity, gender, class and so forth. In considering the media in its international dimensions we also encounter national or regional groups,

---

as a genre in its own right and melodrama as a kind of excessive style in other genres dominates production. Here again the power of emotion in popular media operates as a return of the repressed.

Afolabi Adesanya, a Nigerian film and video maker, provides another, rather startling reason for their success. 'The romance between the Igbos and home videos is perhaps better understood in light of the fact that they are really not moviegoers. The attraction of home video is that the average Igbo man can now afford to provide entertainment in the warmth of his home for his wife and children while he goes off to the stadium to watch a football match.'

Orange Girl
She was an orphan. She was brought to the city for orange hawking. But the situation went sour as she found herself in the wilderness. She has a target. Can an orange seller become someone in life? Find out in this heart wrecking movie.

Take Me To Mama
One mother... two sons
One bomb blast... two lovers
One murder... two brothers at war

Sources:
Jonathan Haynes, ed, *Nigerian Video Films* (Ohio University Center for Research in International Issues 2000).
Afolabi Adesanya, 'From Film to Video' in Haynes, op cit.
Jeremy Nathan, *Nigerian Video*, independent South African film producer (internet posting, August 2002).

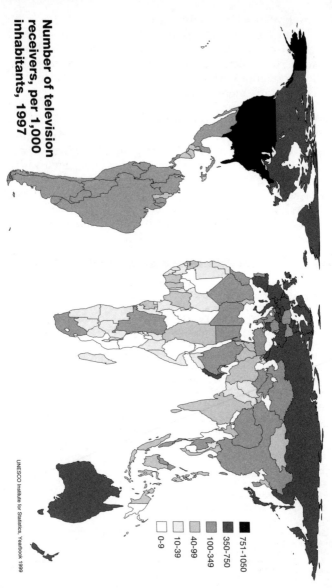

Number of television
receivers, per 1,000
inhabitants, 1997

751-1050
350-750
100-349
40-99
10-39
0-9

UNESCO Institute for Statistics, Yearbook 1999

as well as those who are settled and groups living in transition or as part of a diaspora.

This would seem to be a major factor determining an audience member's relationship with the media. But just as we took care not to generalize about the factors that might lead to an active media user, we should take care not to link any person with only one social category. We all have multidimensional, somewhat floating identities.

Women and men use media forms differently. Hollywood and the magazine industry latched on to this knowledge very quickly by developing genres and promoting stars and celebrities specifically for women. Not only were domestic melodramas, musicals and romance magazines extremely successful but theaters were designed especially to attract women, deliberately cutting out the rougher forms of male culture. Stars and celebrity writers were promoted who had particular resonance with female viewers and readers. Two well-known studies of the TV program *Dallas* and its viewers around the world found that men often ridiculed the show for its American values and its lack of reality, while many women found the dramatic situations emotionally accurate.[14]

The same range of responses appears with differing ethnic, racial and religious groups. Using the *Dallas* example again, one viewer in Israel had this to say: 'I learned from this series to say "Happy is our lot, goodly is our fate" that we're Jewish... I see the characters on *Dallas*: they're almost all bastards.'

Settings

How and why people watch is often determined in group settings such as the home. Most ethnographic studies and anecdotal evidence suggest that when families watch together men and boys control the channel changer. Many women hope to use the TV viewing time as a way of cementing family relationships. They will watch whatever the men or young people want in order to keep the children around or preserve the peace. In some cultures, however TV viewing is predominantly women's space, especially when *telenovelas* dominate the prime time hours. And among some men in traditional cultures TV has been seen as a good medium for keeping women in the home, allowing them to look after children or allowing an escape for men to head for the bars and sports events. In Nigeria, for example, 'cinema-going is predominantly a male activity and, for that matter, an activity for younger, poorer and rowdier males; it is considered of more or less dubious respectability for girls and women.' [15]

A similar male control of the consumption technology cuts across most other media forms, from the 1950s hi-fi enthusiast to the hacker culture surrounding the internet.

Audience studies have taken many forms but divide, into two main types: quantitative and qualitative. Quantitative studies provide useful statistics especially for print, cinema and the internet, but they remain difficult to carry out for the (free) broadcast of radio and TV. A rough criteria might be the numbers of radios and TV sets owned (especially if these are taxed) but in both cases these can be used by one person or dozens, in settings as diverse as an apartment, a school or even a prison.

A further difficulty in measuring audiences numbers, let alone attitudes, takes place in countries or regions where access is limited and where TV viewing and even music listening are group activities. Western media researchers generally conceptualize media use in individualist terms – this makes some sense when 75 per cent of British children have a TV in their rooms. [16] But in Bluefields, Nicaragua, on the somewhat isolated Atlantic coast, as in millions of other communities across the world, neighbors gather in the parlors of those well enough off to own a TV. In fact, the world average for TV ownership is only 23 per cent. But some patterns of access and audience use can be startling. According to the United Nations, more rural Chinese people have access to cable TV than to fixed telephones.

An entire industry of broadcast advertisers has developed the practice of setting specific ad rates for certain programs. The job combines measurement and surveillance. The famous AC Neilsen ratings, culled from their 'People Meters', is part of North American popular culture. The promise of interactive TV may represent a much more sophisticated level of measurement, coupling the computer's awesome ability to record and store personal data and the TV's ability to reach right into the home.

'With interactive television every click of your remote control goes into a database. This is called your TV set's 'click stream', and it can be analyzed to create a surprisingly sophisticated picture of who you are and what motivates you, sometimes called 'telegraphics'.[17]

Qualitative studies also take many forms. They can be conducted in controlled settings or 'in the field'; they can gather data by questionnaire or by direct interaction between a researcher and the 'subjects'. Many of these studies have become controversial and many have striking flaws. Some faults include:

• studies using unsophisticated methods, for example by not sufficiently accounting for the influence of the researcher on people's replies. Research subjects will often tailor their answers to what they think the interviewer wants to hear, or to avoid embarrassment in front of a more educated, or socially powerful researcher. This often occurs in discussions of the popular media, with its 'low class' associations

• studies that seem designed solely to prove the opinions of the researchers

• studies that set out only to measure the bad effects of the media, such as the links between violence on-screen and off. They seem incapable of measuring, or taking account of more positive effects

- studies that set out to discover why some people have anxieties about using media technology while assuming that technology use is good and/or inevitable
- most studies contain a significant bias toward Western models of media reception
- few studies have been designed to look at cross-cultural patterns of media use

This discussion of media effects takes us into the next chapter which will look at the ways in which media and the larger society interact.

1 Raymond Williams, *Culture* (Fontana 1981). **2** Michael Chanan, *Repeated Takes: A Short History of Recording and its Effects on Music,* (Verso 1995). **3** Richard Dyer, *Only Entertainment* (Routledge 1992). **4** Quoted in Chanan, op cit. **5** Raymond Williams, op cit. **6** David Maltby, *Hollywood Cinema: An Introduction* (Blackwell 1996). **7** Silvio Waisbord, *Watchdog Journalism in South America* (Columbia University Press 2000). **8** Raymond Williams, *Marxism and Literature* (Oxford University Press 1977). **9** Scott Robert Olson, *Hollywood Planet: Global Media and the Competitive Advantage of Narrative Transparency* (Lawrence Erlbaum Associates 1999). **10** John Fiske, *Introduction to Communication Studies* (Routledge 1992). **11** RL Gregory, *Eye and Brain: The Psychology of Seeing* (McGraw-Hill 1966). **12** David Bordwell and Kristen Thompson, *Film Art: An Introduction*, 5th *Edition*, (McGraw-Hill 1997). **13** Hall et al, 'Encoding and decoding in the TV discourse' (1973) in *Culture, Media and Language* (London 1980). **14** Ian Ang, '*Watching* Dallas*: Soap Operas and the Melodramatic Imagination*', (Routledge 1985) and Jonathan Katz and Tamar Liebes, *Once Upon a Time in* Dallas (Intermedia 1984). **15** Jonathan Haynes and Onookome Okome, 'Evolving Popular Media' in *Nigerian Video Films* (Ohio University 2000). **16** UNDP, *Human Development Report 2001* (Oxford University Press/UNDP 2001). **17** David Burke, 'A guide to interactive TV', White Dot campaign www.whitedot.org, February 2003.

6 Media and society

*'The strongest argument against modern mass entertain-
ments is not that they debase taste – debasement can be alive
and active – but that they over-excite it, eventually dull it
and finally kill it... They kill it at the nerve, and yet so
bemuse and persuade their audience that the audience is
almost entirely unable to look up and say, "But in fact this
cake is made of sawdust."'*

Richard Hoggart, *The Uses of Literacy*[1]

*'I'd be lying if I said that people don't imitate what they see
on the screen... Of course we imitate. It would be impossible
for me to think they would imitate our dress, our music, our
look, but not imitate any of our violence or our other
actions.'*

Larry Gordon, Producer of the film *Die Hard*

**Media affect media; media influence society; media
reflect society. Chomsky and Herman outline five
media filters reflecting power and ideology. Media
effects: is there too much violence in the entertainment media? Is there enough violence in the news
media? War and peace journalism.**

IN THE PREVIOUS chapter I looked at the ways that
we as individual viewers, readers and listeners and as
members of media audiences relate to the media in all
its diverse forms. But what about the larger, more general relations between the various media and society in
general? In what ways do media reflect or mirror
what's going on in society in general? To what extent
do media influence social trends and attitudes? Is
Hoggart's bleak view the whole story? How do various
sectors of the media industries help create or sustain
power relations in society? To begin to answer these
questions let me suggest three general types of relationship between media and society.

Three relationships

Media influence other media, media reflect society and media affect society. I will look at each in turn; however it is wise to keep in mind that all three types of relation can work simultaneously.

1. Media influence media

All media forms get created from the genres and conventions that went before. No media form, no matter how closely it appears to flow directly from society, stands entirely on its own. There are always as many allusions to other media forms in any single text as reflections of the outside world. Even the most factually-based newscast refers to the conventions of newscasts as a genre. When Homer exclaims, 'D'oh!' at his pesky children he reflects the plight of millions of fathers the world over; yet simultaneously as a fictional character, he also points back in a sort of endless disappearing meta-text of TV fathers since the beginning.

2. Media reflect society

The best way to know what's going on in any society, many people believe, is to study its popular media. Accordingly, social trends, general fears and aspirations, the status of various groups and the power of ruling elites will be seen reflected in the media. When you hear people talking about media as a mirror of society they are framing their comments in this context.

One way of thinking about these issues is to compare similar media forms created in different countries or regions of the world. The domestic melodrama, for example contains similarities across the world but as we saw earlier the Brazilian *telenovelas* and Nigerian video films differ significantly from the US approach. For example the depiction of social class in the Brazilian forms may certainly reflect class as a vital issue in Brazilian society.

Yet, as many have observed the media's mirror usu-

Do women make the news (look good)?

Whilst women are increasingly reporting and presenting the news they are rarely news subjects, according to the results of the most comprehensive overview to date of gender portrayal in the world's media. The study reveals that women account for 41 per cent of the presenters and reporters of the world's news, but only 18 per cent of news subjects.

The report confirms many of the concerns raised over the last decade by women media activists. Women form a majority as TV presenters (56 per cent), but they make up only 28 per cent of radio reporters and 26 per cent of reporters in newspapers. As TV presenters they form a majority in the 20 to 34 year age group but tend to disappear after 50. These facts beg some important questions about employment practices. Just how hostile is the newsroom for women journalists? Is appearance a stronger job prerequisite for women than for men?

Certainly, the international news media is failing to provide accurate coverage when it continues to exclude half of the world's population as news subjects: women featured more in stories on arts and entertainment (35 per cent) or celebrity news (26 per cent). They barely appeared as news subjects in stories on politics (12 per cent), international crises (11 per cent) or national defense (six per cent).

Women's positions and occupations in society reflect stereotypes which should have been left behind long before the turn of the 21st century. Twenty-five percent of all female news subjects had no stated occupation, compared with nine per cent of male news subjects, and 21 per cent of female news subjects were identified in terms of their marital or family status as opposed to just four per cent of the male news subjects.

If women are so invisible as news subjects why are they photographed significantly more often than men? Women accounted for 25 per cent of news subjects appearing in photos as opposed to 11 per cent of male news subjects. Does this, then, support the idea that women continue to adorn news rather than make it?

Source: George Spears and Kasia Seydegart of Erin Research and media expert Margaret Gallagher, *Who Makes the News? The Global Media Monitoring Project 2000* (WACC 2000).

ally works more like a fun-house distorting mirror than one that reflects perfectly.

Power and the media. The media reflect the power dynamics at play in any society. But the media don't simply reflect, they provide the symbols, images, ideas and frames that constitute power itself – the dominant media create some of the forms by which power operates. Not only that, the various media industries now constitute power centers themselves due to their economic clout and central role in communications.

Antonio Gramsci developed the concept of hegemony to explain how power was wielded in the modern State. Hegemony is a form of power or rule not limited to direct political control but one where those who have power maintain their position through the creation of a particular world view, one that seems to be based on common sense. Hegemony doesn't confine itself to intellectual matters or ideas but works within everyday culture and seems to provide a frame for understanding experience.

The various media forms, from the newscast to the blockbuster, don't simply communicate hegemonic ideas that have been created in the board rooms and halls of power, they represent those ideas and ways of thinking in specific media forms.

Society's power holders construct a dominant ideology or way of thinking and viewing the world. This force operates only when the ideas can be represented and communicated. The media are not separate from society; the media are part of it.

Filtering the news. Ed Herman and Noam Chomsky's 'Propaganda Model' in their book *Manufacturing Consent* develops the idea that hegemony is a form of rule that requires the consent of citizens.[2] This consent gets manufactured partially through a filtering process in the news media. They suggest five types of filters:

1st Filter – Business interests of owner companies.

'You've certainly led one of the most extraordinary lives of the 20th century and it's been entirely of your own making. Can you accept the accolade that you are probably the most remarkable Australian in about 200 years?'

– Terry McCrann interviewing Rupert Murdoch in the Murdoch-owned *Adelaide Sunday Mail*

2nd Filter – Selling audiences to advertisers.

'The Coca-Cola company requires that all insertions

are placed adjacent to editorial that is consistent with each brand's marketing strategy... We consider the following subjects to be inappropriate: hard news, sex, diet, political issues, environmental issues... If an appropriate positioning option is not available, we reserve the right to omit our ad from that issue.'

– Memo from Coke's ad agency to magazines.

3rd Filter – Sourcing information from agents of power.

The most cited economic experts in the international press are from free-market think-tank the Institute for International Economics.

Mark Laity, former BBC war correspondent, got so close to his sources that he now works for NATO.

'PR Newswire. The leading source of news from corporations worldwide for media.'

– PR Newswire publicity.

4th Filter – Flak, pressure on journalists and threats of legal action.

Jane Akre and Steve Wilson were fired by Fox TV in Florida over an investigative report on Monsanto's bovine growth hormone in milk. The General Manager of Fox told them: We paid $3 billion for these television stations; we'll decide what the news is. The news is what we tell you it is.'

– www.foxbgh.org

5th Filter – Ideological belief in free markets.

'Buy Nothing Day is in opposition to the current economic policy in the United States.'

> – US news channel CBS rejecting Adbusters'
> 'Buy Nothing Day' commercial which
> called for a 24-hour shopping moratorium.
> (*New Internationalist* 333, April 2001.)

Other sorts of pressures and built-in structures affect how news gets reported and shaped. Racism in the news media, for example, often emerges as a result of social attitudes and pressures on journalists. Several British studies have highlighted a series of reasons why racist stories appear. These include journalist and media owners' personal prejudices; the ethnic composition (overwhelmingly white) in the newsroom; the training of journalists; competition and marketplace pressures to serve the maximum number of readers, which in the West means the white majority; bureaucratic inertia in seeking out diverse news sources; and deep-seated news values that focus on conflict, violence, controversy and deviance.[3]

3. Media affect society

While various theories as to how the media may reflect the larger society provide us with valuable kinds of understanding, it's the debates over media effects that have generated the most heat and controversy. Thus the third customary way of talking about the media is to express concern or admiration over its effects. This discourse of media effects has a long history beginning in its modern form with the birth of cinema in the 1890s and its possible role in corrupting the morals of youth.

Do these types of statements sound familiar when people talk about media effects?

fashion – everyone's wearing those Britney Spears mini skirts

manners – vulgarity in music lyrics leads to increasing vulgar speech among youth

---

Ideology in action – the top ten procedures

Ideology,
1. turns the particular into the universal
2. hides the labor involved, making commodities and cultural texts appear natural
3. sets up false analogies
4. creates a sense of neutrality to mask a particular bias
5. frames the acceptable limits of a topic or issue (sets the agenda)
6. sets up the fallacy that the simplest explanation must be the true one
7. makes the special appeal – leaders as just plain folks
8. confuses the surface appearance of things with the entire phenomenon
9. creates the sense that history leads to this moment and the present situation
10. excels in the practice of TINA – 'There Is No Alternative'

---

fears – excessive violence on TV screens causes viewers to think that their neighborhood is equally violent

behavior – positive images of men as fathers will influence real fathers to take more responsibility

knowledge – hearing one's traditional music on cassette will lead to a rediscovery of the old forms and a greater respect for one's culture

aspirations – when the oppressed people of China see depictions of Western democracy on satellite TV they will become restless and demand change

crime – gangsta rap glorifies gangs and leads to more crime with guns

discontent – the newspaper series on official corruption will lead to a change of government

Keeping in mind the notions of active audiences from the previous chapter, let's move deeper into the discourse of media effects and begin by classifying media effects into three categories: long range, medium range and short range. Long-range media effects shape us as a species or in our overall organization of society. Medium-range effects influence us as members of social groups. Short-range effects work on a smaller scale, perhaps influencing our personal lives.

Making out on the small screen in China

'I used to think that all people in Taiwan were Guomindang [support-er of the Nationalist Government] and if it came to conflict I would be the first one to fight them to the death, but after watching *Special Man and Woman* I have had an about-turn in my thinking. I saw a group of young people across the sea who were just like me, and who strug-gled hard to have a happy life. ■

Correspondent writing to the TV show from mainland China

Here are some typical statements about media effects. Many are firmly believed and probably true. Most remain difficult to prove.

Long-range media effects:

Negative. Media saturation works as an opiate, dulling our senses, making us jaded about the real world. The American Academy of Pediatrics states that children under two years old should not watch televi-sion, saying that TV can hinder proper brain development.

Positive. Cheap and accessible media such as radio, recording machines and cassettes stimulate better communication and new forms of cultural expression for huge groups of people across the world.

Medium-range media effects:

Negative. The media play a key role in racial, ethnic and gender stereotyping, leading to increased tension and misunderstanding about other groups in society. The Canadian anti-poverty activist Jean Swanson refers to the media depiction of poor people as 'poornogra-phy'.[4] One innovative British study, funded by the BBC, of Black and Asian TV viewers highlighted two concerns among the participants about the represen-tations of their particular ethnic and racial groups. Not only did they feel strongly that their poor or non-existent representation would play into the hands of prejudiced members of the white community, they also expressed concern that the images would have a negative effect on their community as well.[5]

Positive. The world media now provide us with an introduction to people and places around the world that we would never be able to visit – thus breaking down barriers to better understanding.

Short range media effects:

Negative. The globalization of media and the voracious appetite of media channels for 'product' leads to a standardization of ideas and cultural forms and to such rapid turnover that style and novelty and the latest thing become ends in themselves.

Positive. 'Let a hundred flowers bloom', said Mao. The proliferation of media forms and channels foster rich possibilities for a proliferation of styles and approaches for art, education and political communication. The globalization of culture makes it possible to draw on artistic talent from anywhere.

Media effects: violence

Violence ranks as the number one controversy in dicussions about the effect of the media. From the new mass circulation newspapers of the late 19th century, and from early cinema's fascination with the chase and with crime and criminals, to today's steady diet of murder and mayhem, critics of the media have stated over and over that film, TV and popular music contain too much violence. Social critics, religious groups and governments often chime in. Indeed, a study by the American Psychological Association stated that the average US child watching TV three hours a day has by the seventh grade witnessed 8,000 murders and more than 100,000 other acts of violence. From the local newscast, to reality cops, to crime dramas, to children's animation, violence functions as the central dramatic tool in telling stories and packaging the news.

Many critics believe that exposure to repeated media violence causes not only short-term and medium-term damage but fosters long-range effects on the

Television addiction is no mere metaphor

'Perhaps the most ironic aspect of the struggle for survival is how easily organisms can be harmed by that which they desire....

Psychologists and psychiatrists formally define substance dependence as a disorder characterized by criteria that include spending a great deal of time using the substance; using it more often than one intends; thinking about reducing use or making repeated unsuccessful efforts to reduce use; giving up important social, family or occupational activities to use it; and reporting withdrawal symptoms when one stops using it.

All these criteria can apply to people who watch a lot of television.'

Robert Kubey and Mihaly Csikszentmihalyi,
Scientific American, February 2002

entire society. Various researchers have argued that general exposure has general effects, such as a jaded view of the world and the tendency to objectify others. Specific exposure can have specific effects, such as the belief that the world is a more, or less, dangerous place than is really the case.

Unfortunately, the debates over violence have been rife with unsubstantiated claims, half-baked theories, rigid opinions based on bias and potent doses of fear. Myths and misconceptions litter the ground. In order to get beyond these problems the US media researcher, James Potter, pinpoints several myths about the effects of media violence.[6] Although Potter clearly carries his own bias, his listing helps to sort out the issues and clear away some of the underbrush:

1. Media violence does not affect me
2. The media are not responsible
3. Children are especially vulnerable
4. There is too much violence in the media
5. Violence in the media reflects violence in society
   Media are only responding to market desires
      lence is an essential element in all fiction
          ing the amount of violence will solve the

9.   hing I can do.

Over the past 50 years researchers have developed four types of research to look into the effects of media violence. The most common research studies have looked at behavioral effects. This usually involves showing people violent images and measuring changes in their behavior, either in a laboratory setting or over time. Some studies have concluded that watching violence on screen provides a 'behavioral script' that might later be used when confronted with a similar situation in life. Others believe that exposure to, and identification with, a violent hero will later provide a rationale for similar aggressive behavior.

Another approach involves desensitization theory. The basic premise here rests on the belief that a steady diet of media violence can lead to lower levels of sympathy and concern for others. One study, for example, concluded that: 'men who watch slasher films containing rape depictions show less sympathy toward actual rape victims.'[7]

A third approach, applying more complex methodology and longer-range measurement, is known as cultivation theory. The proponents of cultivation do not believe that violent media cause violent or aggressive behavior. Rather their theory tries to show how media violence works as a means of social control for those in power. Representations of violence, 'vividly dramatize the preferred power relations and cultivate fear, dependence on authority and the desire for security rather than social change.' The key theorist, George Gerbner, who began his studies in the 1960s and founded the Cultural Environment Movement (CEM) in 1991, believes that a steady diet of media violence can encourage viewers to develop a 'mean world' outlook, sometimes exaggerating the risks in their community. Gerbner argues that 'television violence is the simplest and cheapest dramatic means available to demonstrate the rules of the power game'.[8]

Finally, a limited-effects theory vigorously (I won't say aggressively) counters the first three approaches.

Many of the strongest critics of research into the effects of media violence attack the faults and biases behind the behaviorist studies in particular. Jonathan Freedman, a Canadian media analyst, writes that virtually all the violent-effects studies contain serious flaws. He claims that many of the studies actually show that violent images have no effects but that the researchers are too blind or biased to admit it.[9] Other theorists point to the hidden agendas of the behaviorist researchers, labeling them witch-hunters and moralists. They remind us that much of the early effects research began in the public relations and advertising worlds of the 1950s, where media effects were taken for granted and where the goal was to understand specific effects and behavior triggers in order to sell people more products.

Unfortunately the no-effects approach remains largely negative and can point to few studies of its own. Thus we should ask: 'Do weak proofs and flawed studies mean that violent media produce no effects?'

No matter what the approach, those critics and concerned media watchers who take up the issues of media violence almost always mix their concerns with other agendas. When you hear talk about violence in the media, 'There's usually something at stake, politically speaking, in choosing to adopt one stance over another,' say Cynthia Carter and Kay Weaver writing on the politics of the violence debates.[10]

A rough way of categorizing the people who take up the violent media debates is to divide them into maximizers and minimizers. The maximizers include:

- religious groups of many sorts who often see violence in media as a symbol of declining morals and social decay. These concerns cross many religious paths across the world. In India and some Muslim societies many religious people, not only 'fundamentalists', see violence as symbolic of Western culture and a threat to tradition. The religious right in the US has used campaigns against media violence to attack 'liberals' in Washington and Hollywood.

- governments who have been persuaded to hop on the maximizers' bandwagon, either from a concern that too much media violence could undermine public order or as a handy tool to gain voter attention.
- the advertising industry, which certainly believes in media effects: that's what they base their sales pitches on; violent effects just don't get mentioned.
- nationalists of many kinds who have attacked US cultural imperialism by pointing to the debased nature of US media and its addiction to violence.
- a wide spectrum of left and liberal social critics who traditionally based their critique of commercial culture on violence in the media. Feminists and anti-racism organizations have consistently argued that violence toward them in media representations fosters directly negative behavioral, desensitizing or cultivation effects.

The maximizers thus constitute a very broad category. The minimizers attract a varied group as well:

- the entertainment industry, from Jack Valenti to the multinational makers of video games, officially express concern over troubling social issues, including crime. When pushed to the wall, however, they vigorously argue that the media cause no negative effects. Taking a page from the gun lobby they argue that 'TV doesn't kill people, people kill people'.
- anti-censorship groups, usually led by those with the most liberal attitudes in the society, usually downplay connections between media violence and real violence. Their fear, unfortunately too often justified, is that the state or religious groups will use theories of media violence to limit free expression, minority opinion and political dissent
- some social and political critics on the left fall into the minimizers' camp by dismissing the entire project of concern over media effects. They argue that

capitalism's structural problems of poverty, racism and unemployment pose far greater threats: these are the real causes of crime. Attempts to point the finger at the media, they argue, just provide an easy 'feel-good' target and a distraction from the real issues.

Carter and Weaver argue that we need to move beyond the polarized effects-versus-no effects camps: 'We reject all attempts to force researchers into opposing camps.' (Perhaps, I'm a little guilty of that with my maximizers / minimizers chart.) They also believe that this either / or dynamic reflects a male bias too quick to label critics of violence as 'witch hunters and moral campaigners'. They argue: 'We need to investigate in more detail the extent to which masculinity may be linked to media violence.' Australian media theorist Stuart Cunningham agrees: 'The [media violence] debate has been profoundly masculine in orientation.' He argues that we must 'shift the terms of debate away from the dominant, but limiting, models of free

---

Four types of violent representation

Agreeing on a definition of violence has proved elusive. One person's violence is another's harmless knock-about. One person's gratuitous image is another person's realistic depiction of modern urban life. The US National Television Violence Study (1997) came up with these varieties, especially as they affected children.

1. *Unpunished violence* – 'It is felt that this does not alert young viewers to the fact that violence is wrong and that we should not be violent.'
2. *Painless violence* – '...the message promoted is that violence does not result in serious injury, pain, or death.'
3. *Happy violence* – '...happy violence desensitizes children to the seriousness of violence and tells them that violence is funny.'
4. *Heroic violence* – 'It is said that this kind of portrayal encourages children to emulate violent behavior. Violence used by a good guy for a positive reason...may well be more problematic than violence initiated by a "bad guy" who does not ultimately gain from their violent actions.'

Source: *Violence and the Media,* Cynthia Carter and Kay Weaver (Open University, 2003)

speech and censorship, which derive from masculine ideas of aggressive journalistic realism on the one hand and paternalistic protectionism on the other'.[11]

To move beyond this impasse, write Carter and Weaver, researchers should examine how media violence works to sustain and create structures that legitimize the place and position of dominant groups in society.

Violence and war: 'the one color missing was red'
Is there enough violence in the media?
Surely that's the wrong way to phrase the question, is it not? Isn't the problem one of too much violence? The answer, I think, lies in the type of media we focus on. George Gerbner's hypothesis makes sense. Exposure to violent media in entertainment and in Western domestic news coverage creates a 'mean world' outlook. However, if we shift the focus to look at the representation of war and international conflict, I believe the opposite is true.

When we live with the media, we live in a 'sanitized world' largely cut off from the violence and trauma caused by war, especially wars where 'we' have a stake. Witness the howls of anger and abuse thrown at the Arab satellite broadcaster, al-Jazeera when they dared to show pictures of dead British and US soldiers during the Iraq war in March 2003. In the name of good taste, and possibly the Geneva Convention, the screening of those images was condemned. British Prime Minister Tony Blair and US Secretary of State Donald Rumsfeld expressed outrage and 'horror' at the

---

War! What is it good for?

'...US journalists responded with much enthusiasm to the 2001 bombing campaign in Afghanistan, primarily because it provided them with something "serious" to report.... these journalists were thinking "Oh God! Thank God...a war... It's a real story. It's real journalism. It's a nation challenged."'

New York Times columnist Michael Wolff on CNN, 2001

---

broadcast. But the channel was unrepentant. 'Look who's talking about international law and regulations,' said al-Jazeera spokesperson, Jihad Ballout. 'We didn't make the pictures – the pictures are there,' he continued. 'It's a facet of war. Our duty is to show the war from all angles.'[12]

A survey of British TV coverage of the Iraq war conducted at Cardiff University concluded: 'It is clear that the accusation of BBC anti-war bias fails to stand up to any serious or sustained analysis.' For example, say the survey authors, 'When Tony Blair accused the Iraqi regime of executing British soldiers – a story Downing Street was later forced to retract – the BBC was the only one of the early evening news bulletins that failed to examine the lack of evidence to support it.'[13] Another newspaper reporter summed up the BBC TV coverage of the Iraq war in generally favorable terms but concluded with a concern about the way 'in which broadcast professionalism is converted to stage-managed triumphalism in a period of national combat.[14]

Flashback

In Britain, this cleaned-up picture of dirty wars stretches back to depictions of British troops in the First World War. Casualties on 'our side' were not to be shown in the interests of military intelligence and, of equal importance, lest they contribute to low morale on the home front. At the Home Office, then, there are certainly some believers in the effects of violence on the screen.

When it comes to Western war reporting, Gramsci's notion of hegemony seems too subtle. What we usually experience is a closing of the media ranks behind 'our' troops, 'our' government and 'our' boys. The propaganda machine seems like a better description. The Norwegian Professor of Peace Studies Johann Galtung has developed a 12-point list of important characteristics of media coverage of war. He believes these often contribute to public misunderstandings of the complexities of violence.[15]

1. Decontextualizing violence: focusing on the irrational without looking at the reasons for unresolved conflicts and polarization
2. Dualism: reducing the number of parties in a conflict to two

From massacre to victory

The great war – the editor and the PM

'It was a pity that, in all the recent remembrance of the first world war, there was nothing about the press. In 1917 the prime minister, David Lloyd George, confided to CP Scott, editor of the *Manchester Guardian*: "If people really knew [the truth], the war would be stopped tomorrow. But of course they don't know and can't know." *The Guardian*'s CE Montague described how the wartime truth was inverted; a massacre became, "quite a good day – a victory really".'

John Pilger website, http://pilger.carlton.com

Vietnam – a TV war

'The cumulative effect of all these three- and five-minute film clips, with their almost unvarying implicit deference to the importance of purely military solutions... and with their catering (in part unavoidably) to a popular democracy's insistent desire to view even as unbelievably complicated a war as this one in emotional terms (our guys against their guys), is surely wide of the mark and is bound to provide these millions of people with an excessively simple, emotional and military-oriented view of what is, at best, a mighty unsimple situation.'

Michael Arlen, *Living Room War* (Viking 1969)

Iraq – a cable news war

'The one color missing, for the most part, from the first week of television coverage was red, the primary color of war... "The cable news networks" ratings have shot up many hundreds of points as a result of the war and, even with the sand blowing in their eyes and the war not going as well as they and the White House had led us to believe it would, they weren't about to let go of the adrenaline rush that they had helped fuel. (With banners such as "Showdown Iraq" and "Target Iraq", they had all but said, "Iraq, here We Come!")...

None of them used the weather delay to do any in-depth stories on the history of Iraq, or to discuss the various factions in the country – the Kurds, the Shiite and Sunni Muslims. Instead, they began to hedge their bets on the war, focusing on "the mood of America" and on heartening stories of service and sacrifice. Of course, you can't do a story on the mood of America without showing a TV, so CNN showed a picture of a TV tuned to CNN, with Wolf Blitzer broadcasting from Kuwait City.'

Nancy Franklin, 'News Under Fire: Real-time reporting in the fog of war.' *The New Yorker*, 7 April, 2003.

3. Manichaenism: portraying one side as good and demonizing the other as 'evil'
4. Armageddon: presenting violence as inevitable, omitting alternatives
5. Focus on individual acts of violence while avoiding structural causes, like poverty, government neglect or police repression
6. Confusion: focusing only on the conflict area
7. Excluding or omitting the bereaved: thus never explaining why there are acts of revenge and spirals of violence
8. Failure to explore the causes
9. Failure to explore the goals of big powers
10. Failure to explore peace proposals
11. Confusing cease-fires without actual peace
12. Omitting reconciliation: conflicts tend to re-emerge if no attention is paid to healing fractured societies.

'And there's always a dead baby'

Rune Ottosen of Oslo Univeristy, in his course on war and peace journalism, identifies several key strategies of a military campaign to 'soften up' public opinion through the media in preparation for an armed intervention.[16] These are:

The preliminary stage – during which the country concerned comes to the news, portrayed as a cause for 'mounting concern' because of poverty / dictatorship / anarchy

The justification stage – during which big news is produced to lend urgency to the case for armed intervention to bring about a rapid restitution of 'normalcy'

The implementation stage – when pooling and censorship provide control of coverage

The aftermath – during which normality is portrayed as returning to the region, before it once again drops down the news agenda.

Effects: is there anyone out there?

One cause of bad war reporting in the West may be the declining interest among editors and owners in any sort of intelligent international coverage. In the US and Britain the *Survivor* series, set in Africa, took up most of the air-time for African coverage in 2001! When I asked a Canadian TV programmer a few years back why their network carried so little 'Third World' content he replied that if anything important was happening 'they would send a Canadian crew to get the story from a Canadian point of view'. Here in frank language is the ideology of public broadcasting as a cover for systemic ignorance.

According to a study entitled 'Watching the World,' in Britain only three-per-cent of peak-time programs feature anything about the majority of humanity, and almost all of that is confined to the minority channels. In the media 'global village', other nations generally do not exist unless they conform to stereotypes little different from those of the First World War. The authors call this media representation 'a disaster in the era of globalization'. Their reports show that 'the space for in-depth factual programmes examining the lives, experiences, politics and environment of the majority of the world's people – and allowing them to speak for themselves without mediation – has almost completely died'.[17]

Viewers with ties to the old countries now living in the diaspora feel that lack acutely: 'My children were born in [Britain] and don't know anything directly of Africa. What they see of black people on TV forms a bad picture in their head about the country where I was born,' says 'Yaba' from Manchester in Britain.[18]

We ignore media effects at our peril. When the advertising and public relations industries spend billions to capture our ears and eyeballs, backed up by market research, polling, 'People-Meters', focus groups and thousands of bright Communications graduates, we should probably take the media effects seriously too.

But we're not dummies either. The active audience and the millions of Todd Gitlin's agnostics, content critics and abdicators know that a better media world remains possible, with richer, more creditworthy relations between media and society. The ideas and actions of the media-active form the subject of the final chapter.

1 Richard Hoggart, *The Uses of Literacy* (Penguin 1990). **2** Edward S Herman and Noam Chomsky, *Manufacturing Consent: The Political Economy of the Mass Media* (Pantheon Books 1988). **3** Simon Cottle ed, *Ethnic Minorities and the Media* (Open University 2000). **4** Jean Swanson, *Poor-Bashing: The Politics of Exclusion* (Between the Lines 2000). **5** Karen Ross, 'In whose image? TV criticism and Black minority viewers' in Cottle op cit. **6** James Potter, *The 11 Myths of Media Violence* (Sage 2000). **7** Dietz et al, 'Measurement of empathy toward rape victims and rapists' in *Journal of Personality and Social Psychology* 1992, quoted in Cynthia Carter and Kay Weaver, *Violence and the Media* (Open University 2003). **8** George Gerbner, *Invisible Crises: What Conglomerate Media Control Means for America and the World* (Westview 1996). **9** Jonathan Freedman, *Media Violence and Its Effect on Aggression: Assessing the Scientific Evidence* (University of Toronto Press 2002). **10** Cynthia Carter and Kay Weaver, *Violence and the Media* (Open University 2003). **11** Stuart Cunningham, 'A neverending story? The TV violence debate' in *Media Information Australia*, 1992. **12** Brian Whitaker, 'Al-Jazeera causes outcry with broadcast of battle casualties' in *The Guardian*, 24 March 2003. **13** Justin Lewis, 'Biased broadcasting network' in *The Guardian*, 4 July 2003. **14** David Elstein, 'Caught in the crossfire: broadcasting in wartime' in www.opendemocracy.org 25 June 2003. **15** Cited in Danny Schechter, 'Covering violence: How should media handle conflict?' www.mediachannel.org, 18 July 2001. **16** Cited in Anup Shah, Global Issues website, www.globalissues.org, 2001. **17** 3WE – The Third World and Environmental Broadcasting Project. http://www.epolitix.com/forum/3WE. **18** Quoted in Karen Ross, op cit.

7 For a better media world

'Who is the 'digital revolution' overthrowing? Make sure it isn't you.'

White Dot campaign

Millions of people across the world have no access to media or little choice in what they can see, hear or read. Democratic activists need to make the media a political issue and work on two fronts – within the dominant media and with oppositional forms. Work for international change. Educate yourself.

I HOPE THAT the preceding chapters have captured both the threat and the promise that dominant media represent to those of us working for democracy and social change. I hope also that the contradictions within corporate media, the disruptive potential of new technology and the belief in some level of active audiences provide openings for new possibilities. There is no room for fatalism in thinking about the forms of commercial media and our relations with them. As Raymond Williams reminds us, any moment in social and cultural history combines elements of the dominant and residual, but also the emergent.

This final chapter provides concrete ideas and actions for change. Change can take many forms and emerge from varied situations across the world – from young activists creating new forms of art and communication, to wizened bureaucrats at the UN who refuse to give up on a system of more equitable global information flows. Change can also take place in the sphere of radical, alternative media practiced by those outside the mainstream and in opposition to the dominant. Change emerges from both the production and the consumption ends of the media chain – from the Nigerian video film producers who grabbed the appropriate technology, to personal computer users who demand machines that are user friendly rather than dumbed down.

The missing audience

Let's begin, however, with a reminder. Throughout the book I have talked about large-scale media; media seen, heard and read by hundreds of millions of people around the world. There are, nonetheless, several hundred million more almost totally cut out. Let's pause to remember these missing millions.

No access. Millions of human beings not only have no TV but no electricity; the same numbers not only have no internet but no phone lines. One estimate shows that 50 per cent of the world's people live further than three miles away from a phone line.[1] In many countries entire regions get left behind when deemed too inaccessible, or peopled with groups possessing lesser rights and status. Even for relatively well-off Europeans the high cost of long-distance calling has put the brakes on internet diffusion. For older media, such as cinema, the historic colonial patterns of distribution have prevented non-Western filmmakers from reaching their own local audiences. This is also true in Canada, where Quebecois films must battle for screentime in Quebec. As the Argentine ad-campaign for internet service baldly proclaimed: 'If you haven't got internet, you don't exist.'[2]

No choice. Hundreds of millions of potential audience members have access to the technology but in the words of Bruce Springsteen they often find, '57 channels and nothing on'. Lack of choice stems from state censorship, as in China, Iran and many other countries ruled by religious or political zealots afraid of outside ideas and influence. It can also stem from the de facto censorship of commercial and corporate priorities, where cost-cutting and the single-minded pursuit of the largest audience freezes out diversity.

No respect. Plenty of potential viewers, readers and listeners get cut out or give up in disgust because the dominant media (in its various global forms) provide nothing of substance that reflects their lives or nothing but demeaning representations. Around the world, for example, various ethnic minorities, diasporic communities and Indigenous peoples often find nothing in the dominant media that speaks to their realities; for millions watching TV in the West the main picture remains one of ridiculous or nasty stereotypes not much advanced from their 19th century origins.

No interest. In fact, the dominant media take almost no interest in the majority of the world's population – no interest in international content; no interest in poor people, who don't represent a 'good demographic' for consumption; no interest in old people, a minority that also doesn't spend a lot. Celebrities, the well-off middle-classes and the affluent young: that's the target market.

Is it any wonder that so many have found nothing to interest them in the media – have given up on Hollywood cinema, commercial or State radio and large swaths of standard TV? Even the world of corporate publishing has greatly narrowed the range of titles it sees as profitable to print.

Make the media a political issue

The US media analyst Robert McChesney in his book *Rich Media, Poor Democracy* makes an eloquent plea for political activists to rethink the US media. Too often, he writes, political people think of the media as peripheral institutions, communicating the political content that is made elsewhere or as harmless entertainment. Activists must learn to see the media as situated at the very center of the political and economic systems, for the media industries have grown so large they now comprise a huge economic force of their own. This lack of attention to culture and the cultural industries is a staple of Western left-wing critics of the status quo, but it represents an outmoded picture of society where the economic forces represent the base and culture sits in the less important superstructure, of secondary importance and solely a reflection of the real motors of society.

Political activists in countries outside the US and perhaps Japan, often think of the import of US and Japanese media in nationalist terms. And in terms of the news media, many activists are keenly aware that newspapers and state TV operate as significant political tools for local and national elites. But beyond these issues of cultural imperialism and censorship, activists across the world have failed to develop specific policies on the media.

This is slowly beginning to change and activists have begun to insist that political parties and movements develop positions on the media. For example:

- Should the commercial framework be modified or supplanted by concepts of public service?
- Should state-run or funded media be made democratically accountable and transformed to real public media?
- Is concentration of ownership a phenomenon that can be tempered through anti-monopoly legislation?
- Should cities and regions insist on a diversity of media ownership and management? For example, should one person or company be allowed to own TV stations and newspapers in a single city?
- How far should the state encourage or discourage foreign media? What's the balance between protection of cultural resources and a healthy exposure to international forms?
- Should media technology or its 'software' be directly taxed as in Britain?
- Should journalists and the media outlets they work for accept any social responsibility to the communities they report on; does social responsibility necessarily impair the role of a free press?
- Should advertising and public relations messages be

protected as a form of 'free speech' or governed by product liability codes?

Building the media opposition

The ideas and issues listed above pertain to the dominant media. Just as important should be support and the nurturing of independent radical forms, where social and community activists can talk together directly.

Whether we call this realm, which exists outside the state and corporate realms, civil society or the public sphere, we need to recognize the crucial role of media within it. For example, the Aboriginal media of Australia have fought an uphill battle for many years, sometimes achieving significant victories. Freda Glynn, one of the founders of the Central Australian Aboriginal Media Association (CAAMA), describes the dramatic impact that securing their radio broadcasting license had: 'When we first broadcast, I'd seen women cry when they heard their language on the radio, just so excited and laughing and joking, you know.'

Another key radio station owned and operated by Aboriginal people is 4AAA-FM in Brisbane. 4AAA created a unique format, mixing country and western music with indigenous news and music. That has made the station enormously popular and in the opinion of the managers brought Aboriginal issues to a much wider audience. Tiga Bayles, the station manager, describes their work as an essential service, not just a secondary program or alternative: 'With our country music we are getting into the kitchens, the lounge-rooms, the bedrooms, the cars, the trucks, the taxis. We've got indigenous music, indigenous commentary going into non-indigenous people's space.'[3]

Work for international media policies

As outlined in Chapter Two, the United Nations has long recognized that the need to communicate and gain access to information constitute human rights.

A 12-step program for media democracy
by Jeff Chester and Gary O Larson

Concentration and Control

1. Ownership limits
2. Merger review
3. Spectrum management – the invisible electromagnetic spectrum that carries all the 'new media' should be managed for the public good rather than private interests
4. Privacy protection

Content and culture

5. Intellectual property / fair use / open source – the rights of copyright holders must be balanced with the needs of citizens for information
6. The 'dot commons' online civic sector – non-profit groups must fight for space on the Internet before commercial interests completely take over
7. New media tools of democracy – various types of non-profit web publishing, file sharing, and artistic expression should be celebrated and expanded
8. New support structures for the digital age – large-scale infrastructures need investments of public money

Access and diversity

9. Open access / open architecture – citizens should have the choice of, for example, computer service providers; communication standards must not be monopolized
10. Set-top standards – TV set-top boxes must not become control or surveillance mechanisms
11. Digital television – will the proliferation of new channels allow public media?
12. Universal service – will the new media follow the 'Post Office' model, thus seen as an essential service, or something only for the rich?

Source: www.democraticmedia.org, from The Nation, July 2002.

During the 1970s a number of countries, backed by the MacBride commission, an international group hosted by UNESCO, argued for the New World Information and Communication Order (NWICO). This was necessary, they argued, in order to address the imbalance of news and entertainment flows from the rich countries of the north to the poorer south. In addition to these one-way flows, artists and journalists in the south often found it impossible to reach their own constituencies and others in the south due to the dominance of northern distribution systems. The commission's final document was savagely attacked by Western governments and by the US media lobby.

Veteran journalist Joseph Mehan of Columbia University has written a post-mortem of NWICO. Mehan had toiled for twenty years at NBC News in New York. After leaving the US to join the MacBride Commission he became radicalized very quickly: 'My arrogance, of which I had plenty, disappeared in the presence of Third World journalists like Tarzie Vitachi who spent time in jail and was exiled from Sri Lanka for his stubborn defense of press freedoms. I met many like Tarzie.' Mehan lists four 'Basic Historic Reasons' why the NWICO initiative failed: 'Basic historic reason number one was the sacred devotion of American journalism to its own narcissistic image – a free, capitalistic, private and absolutely-no government involvement model. Basic historic reason number two: American media people do not like and will not tolerate criticism of their work. Nobody can tell the US media what to do and get away with it.

Media activism

Oppositional media take many forms, depending on their origin and the audiences who receive them. The makers and audiences for queer media, for instance, have shown how small-scale festivals, effective distribution and safe viewing situations provide the base for a larger movement. For those who live under repressive governments, such as the Kurds in Turkey, Iran and Iraq, the circulation of banned music cassettes can provide a lifeline of hope for a better world or sustenance for a political struggle.

Mexico's Zapatistas have used the internet to publicize their movement. Inspired by this, media activists in many countries have harnessed the internet to 'create a forum for continual up-to-the-minute reports as well as local perspectives on the issues', as Independent Media Centre activist Ana Nogueira explains. Indymedia makers are using new forms of video, audio and web-based work to develop in the direction of radical change. ∎

Sources: www.indymedia.org
Ana Nogueira, 'Indymedia: wired dissent' in the *New Internationalist* 333, April 2001.

NWICO was filled with criticism of the US media – most of it true. Today the US media is in trouble with its own public. But to hear it from Africans and others who lived out in the boondocks was unbearable... Basic historic reason number three: ingrained American media values seek to simplify stories by emphasizing personality coverage and by only broadly and superficially painting the nature of the opposing groups. Basic historic reason number four: the Cold War. The Cold War was a major factor in the undoing of the NWICO effort – for ironic reasons. It was not that the Soviets were big supporters of the movement; they were not. So they threw in mischievous resolutions and programs designed to shock and outrage the West. This gave the American journalists the opportunity to claim these were the essence of the NWICO.'

The NWICO was 'a cry for help from the Third World', says Mehan. Unfortunately, the US media's hostility to anything approaching NWICO remains as entrenched as ever. However, a number of modest international policy initiatives have slowly emerged. These include the Sustainable Development Media Program at the UN, which works with universities, libraries and NGOs to set up internet capability. 'The great merit', says Mehan, 'is that this effort is much less costly than the old idea of total infrastructure development.'[4]

Another initiative toward fairer international media policies is The People's Communication Charter (see box).

The US video producer and media activist, Dee Dee Halleck strongly supports such initiatives. But her critique of the Charter shows how it could be extended: 'my main problem with the People's Charter is the implicit passivity. This is a document that originated within European social democracy and smells a bit of paternalism in its call for "professionalism" (just who decides that) and restrictions about things that are "harmful" and the need for

The People's Communication Charter

The Charter includes 18 articles. Here are some highlights:

Access. People should have fair and equitable access to local and global channels of communication.

Independence. There must be international assistance to the development of independent media; training programs, establishment of representative associations, syndicates or trade unions of journalists and editors.

Literacy. The right to acquire information and skills... reading, writing and storytelling; critical media awareness, computer literacy; and education about the role of communication in society.

Participation in policy making. Including the right to participate in public decision-making about the structure and policies of media industries.

Cyberspace. All people have the right to universal access to and equitable use of cyberspace.

Harm. People have the right to demand that media actively counter incitement to hate, prejudice, violence and war.

Source: pccharter.net/charteren.html

"healthy" media. Who decides? There is an assumption here about "standards"...

There is little mention of the global resource of satellite paths. To me this is an extremely important area for organizing... no mention of [satellites] for the military and for surveillance for profit.'[5]

Fight for better news practices

Most journalists swear by the code of professionalism, which lives by the ideology of balance, objectivity, impartiality and fairness. As we have seen, however, this exists more often as theory than in the real world. But what if citizens, community organizations and political activists were to take media professionalism seriously? For example:

- What if we were to demand a real wall between the editorial and advertising departments of newspapers, instead of the creeping mix of 'infotainment' now so prevalent?

- What if newspapers were to live up to their codes of practice that constrain invasions of privacy? We might think that celebrities comprise the main targets, but in Britain the Privacy Commission reports that, 'more than 90 per cent of complaints it receives are from "ordinary individuals"... temporarily caught up in some problem with the media.'[6]

- What if we were to demand real fairness in the quoting of opinions and the selection of experts? As the corporate law critic Harry Glasbeek says, 'Why do they always trot out a corporate apologist when I'm interviewed on the radio but never ask me to appear for 'balance' during the business shows?'

- What if Black and Asian people in Europe and North America were asked to comment on general social issues such as healthcare or education instead of being quoted solely on 'racial' matters?

If, as the postmodern philosophers tell us, truth and objectivity are always spoken from a particular social position and bias and therefore impossible, can these not still function as goals to be strived for? And if freedom of expression should be maintained and the need for journalists to probe and ask uncomfortable questions remain worthwhile goals, can it not also be possible that journalists turn that sort of enquiry onto the media itself?

Some journalists and citizens groups have argued that newspapers should adopt what some call 'public' or 'civic journalism'. The idea is that journalists and citizens should realize that they have common interests in finding solutions to society's problems. Newspapers should become advocates for issues rather than 'mirrors' that solely report on the statements of politicians.

Critiques of civic journalism surfaced almost as quickly as the notion itself. Robert McChesney calls it a, 'well-intentioned attempt to reduce the sensationalism and blatant political manipulation of mainstream journalism'. But, he continues, 'the movement completely ignores the structural factors of ownership and advertising.' Yet, the idea that civic responsibility be taken seriously remains a powerful tool for activists trying to educate the public about media bias.

In countries where investigative reporting and watchdog journalism become matters of life and death for both journalists and their sources, the idea of taking news professionalism seriously provides a powerful tool for opponents of the government. In North America, by contrast, what passes for 'investigative journalism' usually pales in comparison by focusing on methods or easy targets of small-time fraud and corruption. In South and Central America journalists have uncovered major cases of state violence and commercial corruption that have precipitated the downfall of dictators and crooks. Watchdog journalism disseminates what someone does not want to be known.

The situation in South Korea provides another model for hope. There, a coalition of journalists and civil society groups, as Aiden White shows, has 'engaged the government and powerful newspaper companies in a high profile dispute over media policy'. He writes in OpenDemocracy that the fight has taken place on two fronts, 'wresting control of public media from the hands of the authorities', and within the private media. 'Among their demands', he writes, were 'calls for parliamentary supervision of top appointments, new rules guaranteeing editorial independence and laws to prevent excessive concentration of ownership.'[7]

In the process Korean television stations became the focus of protests and peaceful occupations and later a number of press owners landed in jail for tax fraud. But the main goal of the reformers is for legislation to, 'preclude corporate and governmental interference in editorial decision-making, increase transparency in management structures and establish legislative support of minority and independent media, especially local newspapers to ensure diversity.'

Educate yourself: don't be a *luser*

Ellen Rose in *User Error*, a wide-ranging book on our relationship with computers, challenges her readers to take responsibility for the 'space between the chair and the keyboard'. Although careful not to blame computer technicians for all our frustrations, she reminds us that some tech people refer to ordinary users as 'lusers' because we ask so many dumb questions: 'Do I need to plug the printer into the box?' or, 'the screen says "strike any key", but I can't find the Any key.'

Condescending language, for sure, but Rose believes that, 'despite our long-standing dissatisfaction with user documentation... few users do more than grumble...We seem content to remain "dummies", reluctantly consulting manuals that tell us what to do while revealing nothing of the inner workings of the systems we use nor, more importantly, of the values and assumptions upon which the systems are based.'

As Cees Hamelink, a leading figure in alternative international media puts it, if we come to understand its potential the internet may allow us to 'move from strategies of giving voice to the voiceless to strategies by which people speak for themselves'.[8]

The Center for Digital Democracy in the US provides a forum for one aspect of computer education.

Its mandate is 'to preserve the openness and diversity of the internet... through the development and encouragement of noncommercial, public interest programming'. To these ends, it aims: 'To promote the development of a new online "commons", a consolidated and more visible space in which the public will have access to a variety of noncommercial sources of information and service.'[9]

Try this at home, kids

International TV turn-off week. Back in 1977 Marie Winn in her influential book *The Plug-In Drug,* suggested that viewers turn off their TVs for one week. Thirty years later her idea still finds proponents in Canada, the US and Britain. Organizers in Britain's White Dot Campaign claim that four million people switched off during their first campaign in April 2001. The campaigners argue that TV rots our mental and physical health and harms democracy because it discourages people from participating in social life. They believe that 'the best way to moderate your viewing is to stop watching entirely for a while'.

They also have a knack of combining a serious critique with humor. Occasionally, however, they get carried into the realm of ridiculous statements such as: 'Children don't like TV. They watch it because they're bored. And television just encourages them to stay bored and keep watching.'

Some advocates of media education criticize the

campaigns as simplistic. What makes more sense, the critics argue, is a solid understanding as to how the media work, knowledge that can be applied 52 weeks of the year. In addition, the all-or-nothing approach, which makes few distinctions between good and bad programming and the somewhat elitist tone blunt the effectiveness of the campaigns.

And yet. Despite the criticisms such experiments seem worthwhile, especially if adults participate as well as children. So, if you call me or email next April don't be surprised if I answer. After all, the tube will be dark and I'll be sitting around with all that extra time on my hands.

Globalizing media studies

Far too often subjects that only make sense when evaluated broadly get confined to a national or regional understanding. And, not surprisingly, this narrow thinking rests with a Western, white male perspective that equates its view of the world with all others. The study of media and communications has certainly reproduced this narrowness. Thus, a primary aim for this book has been to reach beyond what has been termed 'the self-absorption and parochialism of much Western media theory'.[10] For example, in my discussions of the concepts 'dominant', 'genre', and 'audience' I have tried not simply to pull in random, non-Western, examples but tried to conceptualize the terms themselves from an international perspective.

Nearly all of the theory produced in media studies rests on examples taken from US and British texts and audiences, which as John Downing reminds us, are quite unrepresentative countries in terms of their media histories. Media histories in most of the world have been shaped by 'issues of power, the state, endemic conflicts, societal change, the economy, institutionalized racism and ethnic insurgency, secrecy, and surveillance'. But, writes Downing, these have been marginalized in media studies.[11]

It is, of course, a task easier said than done. I have no illusions that the preceding chapters shake loose all the various layers of Western bias and I am conscious that my attempts to produce theory that balances the global and the local remain inadequate. I am confident, however, that the book begins a process of comparative media thinking and I hope that readers will be prompted to question their assumptions about the media worlds that we all live in.

1 Mark Balnaves et al, *The Global Media Atlas* (British Film Institute 2001). **2** Chris Moss, 'The Unconnected' in the *New Internationalist* 333, April 2001. **3** Freda Glynn and Tiga Bayles in conversation with Mick O'Regan, host of *The Media Report,* ABC, Radio National, 10 July 2003. **4** www.idsnet.org/papers/communications/joseph_mehan.htm Accessed 28 February 2003. **5** Dee Dee Halleck, 'The People's Communication Charter' in *Media Channel* www.mediachannel.org 28 March 2001. **6** Roy Greenslade, 'Everybody's business?' in *The Guardian*, 3 March 2003. **7** Aiden White in www.opendemocracy.org 30 January 2002. **8** Cees Hamelink, *World Communication: Disempowerment and self-empowerment* (Zed Books 1995). **9** The Institute for Global Communications (IGC) has also fostered internet activism since its birth way back in 1987. **10** James Curran and Myung-Jin Park, *De-Westernizing Media Studies* (Routledge 2000). **11** John Downing, *Internationalizing Media Theory* (Sage 1996).

BIBLIOGRAPHY

Ben Bagdikian, *Media Monopoly, 6th edition* (Beacon 2000).

Mark Balnaves et al, *The Global Media Atlas* (British Film Institute 2001).

James Curran and Myung-Jin Park, *De-Westernizing Media Studies* (Routledge 2000).

Robert McChesney *Rich Media, Poor Democracy: Communications Politics in Dubious Times* (The New Press 2001).

CONTACTS

NEWSPAPERS AND MAGAZINES
The Guardian, Media section (Britain): http://media.guardian.co.uk
Le monde diplomatique (France): www.mondediplo.com
The Nation (US): www.nation.com
Adbusters magazine (Canada): www.adbusters.com
Jump Cut: a Review of Contemporary Media (US): www.ejumpcut.org
Thunderbird: the UBC Journalism Review (Canada): www.journalism.ubc.ca

RADIO
Alternative Radio
www.alternativeradio.org
B92 'A multi-faceted media house at the very forefront of the transformation of post-Milosevic Yugoslavia's cultural life.' www.b92.net
CounterSpin Fairness and Accuracy in Reporting (FAIR) broadcasts CounterSpin, a weekly radio show. www.fair.org
The Media Report Australian Broadcasting Corporation, Radio National, offering 'essential listening for those who work in the media industry and for anyone interested in the future of the media'. www.abc.net.au/rn/talks/8.30/mediarpt/
World Association Of Community Radio Broadcasters Worldwide organization of the community radio movement. www.amarc.org

FILM AND VIDEO
The British Film Institute Excellent resources for teaching film and media education. www.bfi.org.uk
California Newsreel. One of the best sources for radical film and video. Excellent selection of African films, including many of the best recent Nigerian video films. www.newsreel.org.

* Michael Moore, if you're out there send us your email address.

ONLINE
Al-jazeera www.aljazeera.net
Association of Progressive Communication (APC) www.apc.org
Campaign for Press and Broadcasting Freedom www.cpbf.org.uk
Center for Digital Democracy www.democraticmedia.org
Global Media Monitor http://lass.calumet.purdue.edu/cca/gmm
Guerrilla Girls 'Feminists are funny.' www.guerrillagirls.com
The Independent Media Center 'Established by independent and alternative media organizations in 1999 to provide grassroots coverage of the World Trade Organization (WTO) protests in Seattle. A clearinghouse of information for journalists, up-to-the-minute reports, photos, audio and video footage through its website.' www.indymedia.org.
Interpress Service www.ips.org
The Media Channel The global network for democratic media. www.media channel.org
Open democracy www.opendemocracy.org
People's Communication Charter www.pcccharter.net
Turtle Island Native Network Comprehensive site for North American and Australian Aboriginal media, including TV, radio, newpapers and internet sites. www.turtleisland.org/news/news-media.htm
TV Turnoff Week www.tvturnoff.org
White Dot campaign www.whitedot.org
World Association for Christian Communications www.wacc.org
Voices 21 'A Global Movement for People's Voices in Media and Communication in the 21st Century.' www.comunica.org/v21

Index